Journey of a Grown Up Black Woman
A Mid-life Transformation from Mad Woman to Lover

Susan Harvey

Journey of a Grown Up Black Woman: A Mid-life
Transformation from Mad Woman to Lover

Copyright © 2014 Susan Harvey

All rights reserved.

No part of this book may be reproduced in any written, electronic, recording, or photocopy without written permission of the publisher or author. The exception would be in the case of brief quotations embodied in the critical articles or reviews and pages where permission is specifically granted by the publisher or author.

The author has tried to recreate events, locales, and conversations to the best of her memory. Portions of dialogue may have been recreated based on memory and accounts of the past. The author and publisher assume no responsibility for any errors or omissions. No liability is assumed for damages that may result from the use of information contained within.

> Books may be purchased by contacting the publisher and author at:
> Morlynn Press
> Colorado Springs, CO
> www.MorlynnPress.com

Cover Design: NZ Graphics
Publisher: Morlynn Press

Library of Congress Catalog #:2014910877

ISBN: 978-0-6922345-5-6

DEDICATION

This Book is dedicated to my children and grandchild,
Christopher, Justin, and Jordan Harvey
and Justin Harvey, Jr.

And to my eternal loving friend Fernando, who pushed,
cajoled, and badgered me until I loved myself enough to tell
my story.

CONTENTS

Introduction   1
Fix Me

Part I
MUSINGS OF A MAD WOMAN

Notes on the Journey	7
The Education of a Grown Up Black Woman	11
Musings of a Mad Woman – Been Done Wrong	15
Word	19
The Outer Limits	21
G.B.	25
I am Love/#@!*%	29
Daughter/Mama Drama	33
Unfriends	37
The Tunnel	39
My Sister's Mother	43
The Nature of Life	47
Mama's House	49
Bearers of the Ark	53
Been Done Wrong Revisited	55

Part II
I AM
∞
RE-MEMBERING

I AM Earth	61
The Journey of Gentleness	67
HOW is WHO Sideways	69
The Journey to Re-member and Re-mind	73
Women's Work	77
What If …	81
A Conversation with God—Relax	85
What I Know to Do	89
The World of Other People	93
The Thing About Tunnels	97
The Voices in my Head	101
The Power of Purpose	105
The Journey of Stillness	109
I AM that I AM	111
McDonalds and Me	115

Part III
I AM
∞
HOME

Tomorrow	121
You Know, What's His Name …	127
Save Me	131
Other People's Children (or The Shit that Weighs you Down)	135
Queen of Hearts	143
It's Not About the Man	147
Going Home	153
Afterword A Word from our Sponsor	159
Acknowledgments	163
About the Author	164

Adinkra symbol: ODO NNYEW FIE KWAN

"Love never loses its way home"
Power of Love

INTRODUCTION

FIX ME—THE END FROM THE BEGINNING

What the caterpillar calls the end, the rest of the world calls a butterfly.
∞ Lao Tzu

I am sitting on the floor in my living room, leaning against the sofa. I am sobbing, my chest heaving, hands pressed against my swollen eyes. I cannot take this anymore. I. Cannot. Take. This. Any. More.

"You are supposed to fix me," I cry to God, first angry, then pleading. "Why won't you fix me? I know you see me. I am your very own; you told me so. But here I am, over 50 years old, and my life is falling apart. Again. Still. I am never quite right for anyone; I never quite fit anywhere. I am always too much this or not enough that. I am hurting. I feel so alone. Why won't you fix me so I can just belong somewhere, with someone? So I can just be right, so I can stop being scared. Why won't you help me? Why won't you fix me?"

I am here Susan, God tells me, and I *am* helping you. But I can't. I cannot fix you.

I am so shocked I stop sobbing. God cannot fix me. *God* cannot fix me. How screwed up I must be if God, *God* cannot fix me. I see God in my mind's eye looking warily at me, my life, and shaking Her head sadly. Sorry, Kiddo, I'd like to fix you, I would if I could, but … Some things **even *I*** can't do.

Wait a minute. Is this really God speaking to me, or just my overactive imagination? And if this is God, what the hell? Have I been sold a bill of goods all these years? A thought flashes across my mind. I remember a new friend once asking me about my greatest fear. After thinking for a few seconds, I hesitantly confessed. My greatest fear is that this God business is all a lie, the greatest hoax ever perpetrated upon mankind. Because if that were true, if God is not who She says She is, if this life process that God shares with me is really a lie, I could not take it. I could not live, for life would be meaningless. This I know. And now my greatest fear seems to be coming realized.

"You are God, the Almighty, creator of heaven and earth, King of kings, Lord of lords. You are the Alpha and the Omega, Jehovah, Yahweh, Allah, El Shaddai." I am desperate now. "What do you mean you can't fix me? Why?"

And then I know. I know with a deep divine knowing that this is indeed God speaking to me. For She utters the five words that shift my perspective, change my life forever.

"Why, God? Why can't you fix me?"

Because Susan, *you do not need fixing.*

I start to sob again, and then laugh, and then rage like a mad woman. "Are you kidding me, God? Are you f'ing kidding me? Have you seen my life? Have you really looked at me? Do you even hear me? I am falling apart; everything is falling apart. My life is in ruins. I am supposed to have it together by now. And I am a mess."

God's voice in my ear, in my heart is calm, as God's voice always is. You do not need to be fixed, Susan. You simply need to re-member who you are. Hear me. You *are* my very own. Do you know how much I love you? You are my creation from the beginning, and now we are co-creators of your life. I am not here to fix what I have created. Nothing I create needs fixing. I am here to re-mind you who you are, and to provide you with opportunity after opportunity to decide and create who you choose to be, how you choose your life to be. Do you see? I am not here to fix you or to save you. You do not need fixing, and you save yourself.

I have stopped crying and I am listening intently now. I reach for my journal and begin to write what God speaks in me. This is the journey. These "lessons" or re-memberings are not necessarily in chronological order. Some pre-date this specific interaction with God by years, but all are notations of what I am coming to know in this journey of re-membering, then living; choosing and creating who I am.

I began blogging this journey in 2009. In the five years that have ensued I have completed my master's degree and started and subsequently suspended my doctoral work. I have divorced my third husband, have embarked upon, and am re-membering love within a new relationship, and have started and quit another career. With God I have transformed my life from that of a mad woman to one of a lover, in both the divine and the secular sense (though there really is no difference).

I do not disparage the mad woman that I was. I have learned to love her because I re-member Love is who I am. And I have come to embrace and love every aspect of my being and every experience of this adventure called my life. Even those that have been painful, and wrong, and that have terrorized me. Even the fear, the missteps, the embarrassments, the hurts I dispensed with a smug sense of satisfaction. I have come to love myself enough to forgive myself and others, to let go *of* and let go *in*. And I have come to love myself enough to tell my story, without attachment to outcome, without attachment to the past, and without even attachment to the story.

This is the journey.

Part I

MUSINGS OF A MAD WOMAN

Loving ourselves through the process of owning our own story is the bravest thing we'll ever do.
∞ Brene Brown

NOTES ON THE JOURNEY

Wouldn't take nothing for my journey now.
∞ Maya Angelou

My then-husband tells me some things are better left unsaid. He offers this advice after I read one of my blog entries to him. He solemnly recommends I think about the possible ramifications of these stories on my future. They might come back to haunt me. One of his friends, he tells me, clicked onto my blog after I pasted the link on my Facebook page. He told my husband that my entries were "interesting."

"The word he kept using was 'interesting'," my husband relays to me with concern. This, in my husband's mind, is a grave insult, and he cannot understand why I display no uneasiness about this slight to my reputation and personhood.

I laugh. Frankly, I do not care what his friend thinks about my life or that I share the sordid details with everyone who can read, and I tell my husband so. I tell him to relax; this is not Deep Throat, it is just life. My husband is very concerned about such things. The ugly details of one's life should be hidden, his experiences carefully sanitized as to incur no questioning of his upstanding, unblemished nature. One's reputation should be carefully guarded.

He gets agitated that I do not share his trepidations and tells me that my writings are just "Black woman drama" that only Black women will care about. Hmmmm ...

Since I am trying to be a loving, kind, dutiful wife, I do think about the possible ramifications of these stories on my future.

Maybe after reading this book, his friends will congratulate him on his patience and longsuffering in dealing with me all these years. Perhaps he (my husband) will be vindicated once everyone knows I am a mad woman. Maybe if we get divorced, I will be forced to give him half of the millions I will make from this book because the courts will read a few pages and determine the break up was definitely my fault and that my poor suffering husband deserves remuneration. Maybe the state of Colorado will demand I pay back the unemployment the citizens of this great state are paying me while I am writing journal entries. Perhaps my family will be upset I share details about my mother's nature and life.

I dutifully consider these possibilities. I even pray about them a little. But in the end, I know I must share my stories. Perhaps no one will take notice or care. Or maybe I will be shunned by my friends, my ninety-two year old Auntie, my brothers, the Pope (I was once Catholic), and the order of Nuns who taught me in high school. Michelle Obama might like the book since she is a Black woman so is obviously interested in the drama.

But maybe, just maybe, someone will read about the messy, chaotic, disturbing, nature of my journey of inner healing and will come to realize that God is in the midst of the madness, loving me unconditionally, as I walk, run, crawl and stumble along this path. And maybe they will know that God is in the midst of their madness, and that He makes the journey both a joyous one and a worthwhile one.

I am not ashamed of my journey. At least most of it. I will not whitewash my life to make it more palatable to old Black men or to the dominant culture in America. I will no more hide the darks parts of my nature under a barrel than I will my Light. My madness is part of what makes me who I am.

Steven Covey said we are not humans on a spiritual journey, we are spirits on a human journey. This human journey is rife with dark, scary tunnels and clearings bathed in sunlight. It is marked with potholes, ditches, mountains and forests, calm seas and raging tempests. I pray my way through the tough spots, stumbling blindly sometimes, forgetting who I am and where I am once in a while, acting the fool every now and then, raging and laughing and loving and healing and fighting through, like the mad woman that I am.

Welcome to the journey!

THE EDUCATION OF A GROWN UP BLACK WOMAN

Education breeds confidence. Confidence breeds hope.
Hope breeds peace.
∞ Confucius

I am 51 years old. I'm not quite sure how this came to be, since just yesterday I was 35. And I live in Colorado. I know the details about how this happened, but really, how did this happen? And I am in graduate school. These three facts amaze me. By some twisted trick of time, space and fate, I am a 51 year old Black woman living in Colorado, trying again to educate herself.

This must be an illusion—this should be happening 30 years ago in Baltimore where a freshly "bachelor degreed," less wrinkled, less cynical, more energetic me would be starting a Masters program in Philosophy.

But unless time travel becomes an affordable (okay, free) reality in the next few minutes, I am that 51 year old version of myself, still in Colorado Springs, still trying to wrap my aging brain around online distance graduate study in Adult Education.

But brain atrophy aside, I know, am painfully aware, that this is exactly where I belong, what I should be doing, at this point in my life. At 21, I was clueless. As well as a married, college drop-out and almost cripplingly insecure about being a poor, Black female, with an incurable hereditary disease hanging over her head. I remember being scared—all the time.

Almost 10 years later when I returned to school to complete my undergraduate program, I was still fairly clueless. However, I had developed more coping strategies. I was on my second marriage, had three small children and I was on a mission. My goal was to just get the degree DONE. I was not really concerned about the course content, I just knew the degree would increase my earning ability. In a failing second marriage, I had to be better prepared to provide for my children and myself. And I wanted the credibility it would give me as I developed and facilitated motivational and job readiness workshops.

And I did it, and did it well; I graduated magna cum laude. It was an incredible accomplishment. I had earned the tuition money myself by working on special projects in the evening. I had set my goal and accomplished it. My two older children, then 5 and 4 attended my graduation. A few years later I divorced my husband, bought a house, and single-parented my children in a decent suburb of Baltimore.

And now, at 50+, I'm at it again. Educating myself. It's been more than 10 years since I took the genetic test and learned that I do not have the disease. I'm in a third, and often struggling, marriage. I'm not as scared as I was. My children are grown and away. I have a grandson. Being lousy at corporate politics, I've topped out in my HR career.

I had to decide what to do next. So here I am, educating myself again. This time, I am supremely independent, I have more confidence, and more emotional time and space. And I've learned to be still. I went through an incredible period in my 30s where I was in an extremely social mode. Very networked, very engaged, had parties, belonged to cultural groups, traveled. It worked; until one day it didn't. I was keeping myself socially busy so I wouldn't have to meet myself face-to-face; I was afraid I wouldn't like what I saw. So one day I crashed, had what Merizow calls a "disorienting dilemma." Then I *had* to be still, had to have a close encounter with myself. In true "me" fashion, I followed that period by starting a women's group where we focused on our spiritual and emotional growth. But I digress ...

During that crash period and since, I've learned to be still, to be introspective, to reflect. I've learned to enjoy being in my own company. I've learned to like and to love myself. I am comfortable in my own skin. I've reaffirmed that I can't make it without God.

Now, in this graduate program, I am learning to savor learning. Though my instinct is to just get the degree done with, like I did with my undergraduate program, I'm resisting that impulse. I am learning to really experience learning–to feel it, to internalize the knowledge, to allow it to impact my life. To really savor it, enjoy it, let it roll around on my tongue like fine wine. I had a Philosophy professor in undergraduate school, who, after explaining a concept, would pull his tongue and implore of us clueless students, "Can you get a taste of what I mean?" That was in 1975. Now in 2009, 34 years later, I can finally taste what he meant.

MUSINGS OF A MAD WOMAN—BEEN DONE WRONG

I wrapped myself in anger, with a dash of hate, and at the bottom of it all was an icy center of pure terror.
∞ Laurell K. Hamilton, *Guilty Pleasures*

I am very conscious of my need to liberate myself from righteous indignation. I have a Black woman's need to be wounded (metaphorically speaking), victimized by my man, and to overcome in a burst of virtuous glory. I have a need to be loved, cared for (emotionally and perhaps, physically), protected. And I have a need to be respected, done right, or all hell will break loose.

This is my third marriage, and I am no closer to understanding myself in relation to my husband than I was 30-some years ago, when at barely 20, I jumped the broom with husband #1. Well, perhaps a bit closer ... Through a relatively recent conscious practice of critical reflection, I am learning to question my knee-jerk reactions to relationship issues. But I have not yet been able to take the next step and to actually adjust my behavior to reflect my new-found enlightenment." Okay, Susan. Feel what you feel, get mad. Then let it go and move forward." As Colin Powell says, "Get mad and get over it." But I can't.

I hold on to this anger, wear it like a badge of righteousness. I think about it, reflect on it, but I just can't take that step of letting go. I know I'm on my way; but I also know that I resist, resist, resist the urge to release my righteous anger. I wear it like it is the proud mantle of Black womanhood. If I allow the transformative power of reflection-in-action to free me, if I dare relax my clenched shoulders and fists and allow the robe of Black woman superiority (insecurity?) to fall around my ankles, then I will stand exposed, naked, vulnerable and guilty, like Eve in the Garden, who didn't trust her experience of God within her to keep her free and mighty and righteous without the sacrifice of blood.

I am a Black woman. I am powerful. I am angry. I am angry with my Black husband who will not/cannot save me. So I must save myself. Again. And I am angry.

Where does this come from? Partly from my experience of my mother who was also a powerful (frightened?), angry Black woman, and who encouraged me to be so. But where did that come from? From her experience of her mother, who was also a powerful (insecure?), angry Black woman. And where will it end?

My daughter, at 23, resists my attempts to indoctrinate her with my just under the surface anger and my been-done-wrong attitude. "Mom, you know you're wrong," she calmly chastises me as I almost plead with her to understand my point of view, to take my side. At her age and beyond, I was the same way with my mother, refusing to accept her anger as my birthright. And I swore, as my daughter does, that I would never behave in such fashion.

I am a powerful Black woman. I'll get there. Hang with me on this journey.

WORD

The Yogic sages say that all the pain of a human life is caused by words, as is all the joy.
∞ Elizabeth Gilbert, Eat, Pray, Love

For the first seven years of my life I was the middle child. And dark. Darker than my sister one year older than I, and my brother, one year younger. Darker than my mother. As dark as my father.

And one day, as I pouted for some reason in the corner near the basement door, my father laughingly said to me, "You sure are ugly." And I realized, right in that moment, that I was. Ugly.

My father had been my ally. My mother and I were often at odds, seemingly since I could talk. My father would come to my rescue, telling my mother that she treated me differently because I was the child who looked like him. And now he had betrayed me. I was ugly.

My six year old heart broke.

Even now, almost a half century later, I have not forgotten that watershed moment in my young life. Almost fifty years later, thinking about this incident, the pain still catches in my chest and I must reason myself past the tears. He was just kidding. He told my mother so when she chided him for his offhand remark. He was sorry.

But I, even then tending toward melancholy, folded in upon myself like a morning glory closing itself to the bright sky. And it has taken me over four decades to unfurl—to open myself once again to the light, to the truth.

I do not blame my father, long gone from this world. He did not know the power of his declarations over my young life. He did not know that at six years old, my belief in the words of others was stronger than my *knowing* my own truth. He did not know that I closed myself tightly.

And it is now, just now, in the third chapter of my life, that I am finally unfurling. Opening myself to my truth, and affirming it out loud. I am love. I am joy. I am beautiful.

I no longer choose to be closed, protecting myself from others' declarations over my life. As Rilke says in *Love Poems to God*[1]:

> *I want to unfold.*
> *Let no place in me hold itself closed,*
> *for when I am closed, I am false.*

This journey is a journey of opening ourselves to our own truths. And I am so sorry for the careless, false words I may have spoken to my children over the years. My loves, open yourselves to truth. Your truths.

---

[1] Rilke's Book of Hours: Love Poems to God. I, 13. Anita Barrows & Joanna Macy, trans. New York: Riverhead Books, 1996, 2005.

THE OUTER LIMITS

Here is the world. Beautiful and terrible things will happen. Don't be afraid.
— Frederick Buechner, *Beyond Words: Daily Readings in the ABC's of Faith*

I drove the car gingerly, carefully, as recently licensed drivers do. My boyfriend, soon-to-be husband, sat in the passenger's seat. He could not yet drive, a curious situation for a nineteen year old Black man in Baltimore. He would not learn to drive for years—after we were married and built a home in the suburbs, and after I became angry about chauffeuring him to business meetings and waiting in parking lots to drive him home again.

We were young, and naïve, and afraid, somewhat misfits. He wore a necktie every day to classes during our first year in college. I was skinny, and poor, and thought people could see the death on me because so many of my family members were dying from a hereditary disease. We were insecure; both of us. We didn't know, as my mother tells it, "our heads from a hole in the ground."

We were driving in the Baltimore area scouting apartments for our first living experience as a married couple. I remember driving slowly west on Liberty Heights through the city, until we came to the event center marquee on the right side of the road. I froze, panicked, almost stopping the car in the street.

I had worked in that empty theatre, turned lunch preparation facility, for a summer during high school. Along with other poor Black students, I was on the assembly line, packing lunches for more poor Black kids in summer programs throughout the city. Since I was not a trouble-maker, I was often given the coveted position at the head of the line, cracking open and placing the empty cardboard lunch boxes onto the belt, setting the pace for the others to drop in their components—sandwich, salad, banana, cookie, napkin, milk.

I took two buses to get to that facility, but had gone no further down the road. And though it was still in Baltimore city, it was the end of my known world. Beyond that empty event building yawned the White world. I had been there, but only as a guest, escorted by my White friends or their parents who lived there. Their modest, separate homes and their clean, wide streets twisting away from the main corridor where buses ran seemed grand to me. I had never ventured into this White world west of Baltimore on my own.

My mother did not drive and my father had become too ill to do so during my high school years, so I took city buses wherever I went. And with my father unemployed, we could not afford a car, anyway.

Riding buses was not unusual for poor Black kids in Baltimore. But since my middle-class White friends did not live near bus lines, they had to come into the city to pick me up for sleepovers or movie dates. Sometimes my mother would ask and pay a relative or neighbor to drive me to them and to evening events at the mainly White Catholic high school I attended.

I was embarrassed about this, our poverty. And insecure. I promised myself I would always have a car so I could drive my future children everywhere without having to beg rides. I swore my kids would go to real doctors' offices with bright waiting rooms, like on television, instead of foreboding-looking state hospital clinics where they would feel small and humiliated like I had felt. My children would feel secure and confident.

But I had no experience in these areas yet.

Just a few miles from my home, I had come to the limits of my universe and I was terrified. I had been away to college for a year, dropped into a foreign world in rural Indiana, and I had come back home wounded from the experience. But this was different.

I can still feel the panic in my chest. Once we passed the event center, we were in uncharted territory. I began to breathe heavily, hyperventilating. "We have to turn around! We have to go back!" I fought the urge to slam on the brakes. My soon-to-be-husband glanced over at me amused, mocking. He certainly would not admit his fear. "What's the matter with you? Just keep driving." So I did.

On that day in 1977, I tensely gripped the steering wheel and crossed over into the unknown world.

G.B.

Sometimes I think there's a beast that lives inside me, in the cavern that's where my heart should be, and every now and then it fills every last inch of my skin ...
∞ Jodi Picoult, *Handle With Care*

Recently, in the midst of a heated argument, my husband called me a "ghetto bitch." I was somewhat surprised that he did so, since he is not generally inclined to name calling or expletives.

He *is* inclined to the convenient memory failure and obtuse verbal and mental flailings that men can affect during arguments. "Huh? What? What do you mean? I have no idea what you mean? Uh ... I don't remember that. Well, you see first you came in the room, and then you said ... and then I said ... and then ..." This enrages me. Generally a very smart man and brilliant communicator, he takes on the mentality of a kindergartner when embroiled in a marital spat. He of course, alternates this with flashes of clarity, when he tells me that I am getting upset over nothing. Again …

I had been in his face. He is a six-foot-four-and-a-half-inch Black man, and I, defiant, outraged, and shrill, was forehead-to-chin with him. Who did he think he was, who did he think he was talking to, he would not control ME!

In all honesty, I had called him ten or eleven good names (with appropriate expletives) before he got in that one. I had also shoved him a time or two, invoked the wrath of God, and loudly wished for his demise. Not my best Hallmark marital moment.

After that memorable conflagration, I retreated to my sanctuary and engaged in deep self-reflection. I am not generally inclined to name calling or expletives either, unless we are engaged in an argument.

What's this all about, this hyper reaction in arguments with my husband? They could escalate into full-scale warfare, where I am shouting, he is angry and belligerent, I call him a few names—you get the picture. These arguments for me are war and I will not lose. Something in me is triggered and I go into emotional overdrive. Then the gloves come off, and it's "on." (Black women know what I mean when I say, it's "on"). My fight-or-flight instinct takes over, and this sister will not flee.

Perhaps this comes from witnessing my parents' arguments, which, at least to my uninitiated eyes and ears, my mother never lost. My father could never best her in a verbal confrontation. Maybe this is because he had a tenth grade education and she had completed a year or two of college, or because he had a much milder disposition than her intense, tough woman persona. Or perhaps because she could be just plain mean when she felt she had to. As I think about it, I was witnessing the fight-or-flight instinct in action. And there is no way she would take flight.

Once, during a drive in our family's Chevy II (before my father became ill), my parents had a terrible argument. Upon returning home, my mother retrieved our sharpest kitchen knife and placed it in a glass of water in plain view on the dining room table. Apparently you placed knives in glasses of water to sharpen them, the insinuation being, of course, that she was preparing for a physical battle. I cried, afraid she would kill my father. After another heated argument, she prepared my father's plate and put a box of mouse poison on the table beside his place setting. She sat staring at him as he ate, totally ignoring her. She once told me, in justification for her madness that if she had not been so tough my father would have run over her, controlled her—something I cannot imagine. And a justification I now use about my argument behavior with my husband. If I do not fight back he will control me, and I will NOT be controlled.

My mother once told me that I was the weak one among the family's tough women, and that the men in my life would always run over me. Apparently I have proved her wrong. I have become as relentlessly tough and borderline violent in my marriage as she was in hers. And I do not like this about myself.

In my defense, I tried to avoid this argument with my husband. He asked a question and I answered in an honest and rational way. I knew my answer would upset him. When he demanded clarification, I refused, telling him further discussion would only lead to one of our arguments.

When he persisted, it was on. My fight or flight instinct kicked in and I then would not back down. I became my mother, eyes locked with his, toe-to-toe, shouting, mean.

In my mind, I am a sweet, kind, supportive wife. I am also perpetually thirty-eight (my good year), a size six and look like Halle Berry. So much for my mind.

In reality, I am afraid. Afraid that I am those aspects of my mother that I did not like and that frightened me. Underneath, however, I suppose I am more afraid I am not like her, and that I am the weak one who will be run over, controlled by my man.

Since I am aware this is an inherited fear, and not a rational one, alone in my sanctuary I pray. I pray that I am that kind, sweet, reasonable person submerged beneath the madness. I nightly recite my affirmations: "I am Love; I am kind and caring; I am in a loving, harmonious relationship with my husband." And I ask forgiveness for calling my Arkansas-born husband a "bald-headed, corn-pone eating, backwoods, 'bama son of a …"

And once God has finished laughing, he forgives me. Because He knows the real me underneath it all, and loves me.

I AM LOVE/#@!*%

To be fully seen by somebody, and be loved anyhow - this is a human offering that can border on miraculous.
∞ Elizabeth Gilbert, *Committed: A Skeptic Makes Peace with Marriage*

My husband and I have been having a conversation about something we want to do together. As usual, we are on different pages.

My instinct is to say "Just forget it. You do what you do and I'll do what I do." And I do say this. This is how I behave sometimes: when we don't seem to be getting anywhere relatively quickly, I emphatically pronounce our inability to work together, and declare separate paths. I am impatient with my husband. Typically a brilliant communicator, in marital conversations he seems vague, fuzzy. I am quickly frustrated with him.

I repeat, "You do what you do and I'll do what I do."

"You always say that," he calmly replies. "I know we had this conversation once. So, let's have it twice."

I have to admit this is a good answer. He is calm. I am relatively so.

But inside, I swear I am having a schizophrenic episode. Half my brain is forming the words I really want to say to him. The other half is chanting, "I am love. I am patience. I am love. I am patience." I wonder which side will win.

Conversations with my husband make me crazy. Or more accurately, I make myself crazy when having conversations with my husband. I am direct; I say what I mean and mean what I say. He is more circumspect and ambiguous. And he has a way of feigning confusion that makes me want to leap across the table and … (I am love. I am patience).

Anyway, the conversation ends pleasantly. We come to terms with the situation at hand. Later, I go to him and kiss him.

Wow! This I am love, I am patience, stuff really works.

I no longer feel my husband and I are perpetually on the edge—one heartbeat away from imploding. Love wins the war in my head more often than not, no matter which of us is being unreasonable. And I am learning to accept that we simply have different communication styles.

I used to ask God why, why, why my husband is the way he is, hoping God would commiserate with me. God, being God, simply said to me, "His stuff is between him and me. How about we deal with *your* stuff"?

A sister can't get a break.

Now, for the most part, I do deal with my stuff and leave his stuff to him and God. I have stopped trying to love my husband, or anyone else for that matter. I have learned that I AM love. And only love can flow from me because love is who I am. I no longer try to do, I just BE. Not that I am perfect at this yet. Though I affirm who I am daily, sometimes I forget and must re-mind myself.

But this I know—God is love. And I am in God and God in me, so I am love. I no longer try to love, I AM love. And this has made all the difference in my marriage and in my life.

I love this journey.

DAUGHTER/MAMA DRAMA

In search of my mother's garden, I found my own.
∞ Alice Walker

I have a complex relationship with my daughter. At 25, she is brilliant and beautiful and headstrong, tenacious and stubborn, and has always been a bit different. At one moment a consummate hippie desiring to live "off the grid" on the side of a mountain; at another moment, angling for a pink leather Coach purse. She runs a small independent record label, is a journalist, a social media specialist, promotes and books bands, and has traveled on her own, living in Denver and LA and New York. She went to college at 16, and I am in awe of her talent and courage and sheer chutzpah. She is a giving and caring person.

And she is a study in contradictions. She teeters between "Mommy can you send me money?," and indignantly declaring to me (with great drama and attitude) that she is "grown," often in the same conversation. I don't know whether to treat her as an adult or as a child. And I often screw up about in which situations I should expect (and demand) adult behavior of her and at which times it is acceptable for her to relapse into pre-teen dependency and attitude and rage.

There are moments when I want to hold her in my arms and rock her as I did when she was a frightened child. And others when I want to order her to grow up and take responsibility for her life. And others still when I am one second from dragging her disrespectful behind from my car and beating her in the street.

She makes me crazy. She knows more than I do, can be demanding, tells me I have ruined her life, and recently threatened to sever all ties with me. Our personal encounters often end with one or both of us in tears.

This would feel tragic except I am struck by the similarity to my relationship with my own mother when I was my daughter's age and beyond. I felt my mother disrespected *me*. After all, I was grown. How dare she try to tell me anything. Of course my mother helped me financially and otherwise as I struggled to single parent my children after my divorce. I don't know how I would have made it without her. And my kids and I lived in her home while I finished my undergraduate degree. But, hey, I was GROWN. And if she didn't start treating me right I was going to have to never speak to her again!

I smile as I am writing this, and I am sure my mother is doing the same from heaven. Thankfully, I was never forced to sever ties with her!

Here's what I am learning:

A. The law of reciprocity (what goes around, comes around) really is true. I am going through the same challenges with my daughter that my mother experienced with me.

B. Family relationships are sometimes hard, but you never give up on each other.

Though my mother had every right to do so, she never stopped trying to give me the benefit of her wisdom. And she never told me what she should have; that since I was GROWN, to go handle my business on my own. When I got too disrespectful she threatened to kill me, though my hair was nearly as gray as hers. But she loved me unconditionally, as I do my daughter. And when I had the nerve to try to end contact with my mother, she just continued to call me as usual, ignoring my craziness.

My prevalent thought when my mother died was a selfish one. It is difficult for me to articulate how vulnerable I suddenly felt. Though our relationship was a tempestuous one, I knew she covered me with her prayers. Without that covering, I felt the mean, mean world could have its way with me. I felt exposed, defenseless. I no longer had accepting arms I could always run to or a person who loved me without question.

But that was before I really understood the depth of a mother's love.

If my daughter severs all ties with me and moves her future family to some foreign country to be away from me as she threatens, my love will always find her. Like God's love for us, nothing will separate her from my love for her. My love and I will never give up on her, on us. And I will always, even from heaven, cover her with my prayers.

My mother was not always right and neither am I, but she loved me. And difficult as I was, she tried to understand me. And she did the best she could to care for me and to help me and to keep me safe. And I do the same for my daughter, for all my children.

This journey is a journey of love and love is about relationships. And though it may not seem so at times, love never fails.

UNFRIENDS

Growing apart doesn't change the fact that for a long time we grew side by side; our roots will always be tangled. I'm glad for that.
∞Ally Condie, *Matched*

*I*t was bound to happen, but for some reason, it took me by surprise.

The phone call from my daughter was a welcome one. After weeks of tension, of hurt feelings and jangled nerves, we were finally back on speaking terms. I whispered a prayer of thanks that our relationship was healing. And then, "Mom, I'm sorry, but you are no longer connected to me on Facebook. It's best for our relationship. And for me. My staff did not need to see the things you sometimes post about our relationship in your blog."

I automatically murmured my assent, "Okay."

But, wait, what? Did I understand her correctly? I was being unfriended?

Unfriended—the ultimate social media insult. The internet equivalent of being dissed. The web 2.0 version of being given the finger.

My child actually unfriended me. Unfriended *me*; her own flesh and blood; her maternal progenitor who brought her into the world in pain and suffering.

Oh no she DI'NT!

At the end of our conversation, I hung up the phone stunned. I was at first wounded, then incensed. I wanted to unfriend her right back. But, I am the mother. I am the mature one. And I can't remember the instructions she once gave me on how to do so.

Damn old age.

My daughter is actually the social media consultant for my business, and I can just envision my next to-do list for her:

    1. Create a Pinterest site
    2. Update my LinkedIn photo
    3. Unfriend yourself

Just doesn't quite have the zing I imagined.

It seems as if I must endure the remainder of my life being unfriends with my daughter.

In the wise fashion of matriarchs all over the globe, I know there is a lesson here. I know I will grow personally, spiritually from this experience. I know my wounded heart will heal. But I also know to embrace the moment. And right at this moment, all I can think of is:

OMG, the little hussy unfriended me! SMH.

THE TUNNEL

It was like trying to see a shadow in the dark.
∞ Melissa Andrea, *Flutter*

The night before I was to hear the results of the genetics test, I thought I would die. Right then. I thought I could not, would not survive the excruciating fear that gripped me as I struggled alone to make sense of an impending fifteen year sentence to advancing dementia, physical withering, perpetual care, and finally death. I had witnessed this sad and frightening process in my father, sister, brother, uncle, grandmother. Their declining ability to control their movements, their speech, their bodily functions. The fear in their eyes when they could no longer speak, then acceptance, then surrender.

The night before I was scheduled to get the results of my own genetics test for Huntington's disease, the hereditary disease that killed them, I was terrified. It had been a few months since I had given the blood sample that would be tested to determine whether I would have the disease and I had, frankly, pushed the whole process to the back of my mind. I recently received the call that the test results were in and I was scheduled to meet with genetics experts at Johns Hopkins tomorrow. I was instructed to bring someone with me.

On this, the night before the meeting, I was in anguish. Alone, in my living room, the terror and grief pressed my knees to my chest and my forehead to my knees in a fetal position; left me gasping for breath on the floor, writhing in emotional pain. Crushed my chest to my backbone, my heart pounding in my spine; then ripped me open exposing the deep places within. I was terrified for myself and for my children and for their future children. I thought I could not, would not make it through the night. The fear felt as if it would explode in my chest, so powerful my body could not contain it, and I would be found in pieces stuck to the ceiling and walls of my lovely living room, the victim of an internal terrorist's blast or spontaneous combustion.

Every protective mechanism within me then kicked in, fighting to keep me safe, fighting for my survival: "It's okay. You don't have to hear the results. Cancel the meeting tomorrow morning. Don't go. You've made it this far without knowing. You do not need to know. Don't go. Save yourself from this pain. Don't go."

I was comforted by this thought, felt the adrenaline pumping in my veins, pounding in my chest, subside a little. Yes, I can change my mind. I don't have to go. I will call first thing in the morning and cancel the appointment. I slept fitfully that night, arms wrapped protectively around myself on my sofa, waking periodically to cry.

When the morning sun streaming through my east-facing living room windows awakened me, I lay still for a long time. I thought I was alive, but I wasn't sure. I felt no fear. I felt as if I had come through a long tunnel. It was very dark in the tunnel, and frightening. Creatures that I could not see skittered across my feet, grabbed my clothing, pulled at my hair. I wanted to turn back to where I could still see the light from the opening into which I had entered. Ahead was darkness. The tunnel was clammy and dank and smelled of decay; I could hear frightening whispers ahead. I was very afraid, but something kept me moving forward. I was desperate to turn back, but I knew the answers, my future, my freedom lay ahead. I hated it in the tunnel, but I had to move through it.

The sunshine that morning told me I had made it through the tunnel. Now I felt—nothing. Numb. My mind felt blank as I prepared for the appointment. I was on automatic pilot. I did not feel fear or anxiety, though I do not remember feeling especially at peace. I felt nothing. Empty. I had made it through the night, through the tunnel of fear. And right then, that was enough.

MY SISTER'S MOTHER

If you have a sister and she dies, do you stop saying you have one? Or are you always a sister, even when the other half of the equation is gone?
∞ Jodi Picoult, *My Sister's Keeper*

My sister is dying. Of course we are all dying, but she is withering in the advanced stages of Huntington's disease. We have not been close, my sister and me; ten and a half years and different mothers separate us. She was beautiful, and ebullient, and loved life; many years ago. When I last saw her, six or so months ago, her halting gait and tortured speech reminded me of the same phase that my sister, Pam, one year older than I, and our father went through before they succumbed to the disease.

Now my sister is in a nursing home and we can only look back fondly to the days when she could walk and talk, however difficult those functions were. Now I am told she sits near the nurses' station where staff can keep an eye on her. Her frequent stubborn efforts to get out of bed have resulted in several falls, so the nurses keep her nearby. She is angry, sometimes refusing to open her eyes or acknowledge visitors' presence or utter the few sounds she can still make. Her mother, now 84 years old, could no longer care for her at home, and takes three buses each way to visit her in the nursing home three days a week. She is tired, and my sister is angry, and I am sad and guilty. Her mother tells me she is going on a trip next week, a short visit to her sister's house in Virginia Beach. She hasn't been out of the house, except for my sister's doctor appointments for a long time.

My sister's son, who lived with her mother and her, moved away several months ago, worn out and depressed, I am sure, by the consuming presence of death and reminder of mortality his mother represents. In his early thirties I am sure he needs to breathe, to experience the lightness of life that exists just beyond the dark, stifling burden of a long decline and lingering death. Though his grandmother tells him he will not have good luck because he neglects his mother, I understand his need to escape.

So my sister's mother was left alone to shoulder the burden of my sister's care, and it was eventually too much. My sister began to fall and her mother could not keep her safe. Though my sister's mother is "elderly" by age, she does not seem so in reality. She seems strong, like my mother was, capable, a "do what you have to do" woman. On the phone with her today, however, with my sister in a nursing home, she seems fragile, vulnerable, exhausted. The men—her son, my sister's two sons, and even our brother who still lives in the same city—do not deal well with my sister's illness and impending death. They avoid her. Men cannot handle what a woman can handle, my sister's mother tells me. We women do what we need to do. We are sad, we hurt, but we do it anyway. We are strong.

I cannot imagine losing a child. My mother buried two children, lost to this disease, and a husband. She, like my sister's mother seemed so strong, superhuman. But they just did what women do. We care for our babies relentlessly, determined to keep them safe, no matter what. Then we tuck them into bed at night, and kiss them, and send them home to God.

THE NATURE OF LIFE

Only yesterday I was no different than them, yet I was saved ...
∞ Gibran Khalil Gibran

I wept, grief stricken about them one evening a few weeks ago. I had not cried about my deceased family members for years. My sister, one year older than I; my brother one year younger; my father and his brother and their mother; an older sister that I never knew. All dead from Huntington's Disease, an hereditary disease in our family that took them, but for some reason, spared me.

I remember flying to or from a business meeting some years ago. As I peered out of the plane's window, a spectacular sunset painted the sky pink and orange and purple. Tears welled in my eyes—for the beauty of the scene and for my sister and brother and father who never got to see such an incredible sight from 30,000 feet. Who would never see something this beautiful.

I do not remember what triggered my recent thoughts about Pam and Terry and Daddy and Uncle Arthur and Mother Bea and Linda. I do recall that I knew I had not yet resolved my feelings of guilt and unworthiness around their dying and my living. Especially about my sister, Pam, with whom I was closest, with whom I shared a room until I grew up and moved away. Who would come over to my twin bed in the middle of the night and push the covers away from my face because she was afraid I would suffocate in my sleep. Who was smarter than I, and stronger, and more talented, and loved God more than I did. Why was she taken while I lived.?

And then I felt that still small voice of God speaking to me. Why are you crying for Pam, for them all? *They* are fine; I've *got* them. They are with me. They are not struggling or in pain; they are safe and in peace. The question you must deal with is not why they are gone, but why *you* are still here? Who you are and how you are and what you are to be about. You deal with *your* life. They are taken care of. They are in joy. Leave them to me; now let's talk about you …

The journey continues.

MAMA'S HOUSE

She is the one we leave home to look for. She is the one we come home to.
∞ Clarissa Pinkola Estes, *Women Who Run With the Wolves*

My parents purchased the little row house in a transitional neighborhood in Baltimore city in 1963, when I was almost five years old. Pandemonium had broken out several years earlier when the first Blacks purchased houses here, crossing the nearby bridge separating this neighborhood from the "inner city" to the east. Our next door neighbors were White and I remember our families hunkered down together during the '68 riots. We tied a black scarf on our car antennae to indicate we were a black family, sort of like the Jews in Egypt, and our car was passed over by the rioters. We tied a black scarf to our White neighbor's antennae also.

My father, I am told, wanted to continue looking at homes, but my mother fell in love with the shiny hardwood floors in the house and the mature trees lining Denison Street. This was the first home they owned together, a starter home from which to launch a promising family life. They never intended to live there forever.

But then, life happened. Or rather, death happened. A genetic disease robbed my father of his health, his ability to work, and eventually, his life; and relegated my mother to decades of caring for him and their dying children. Without income, living on government assistance, my mother fought to hold onto that increasingly ragged little house in, what had become, a rapidly declining neighborhood. What was initially a starter home in a decent area just over the bridge from the inner city, had become an albatross of sorts in a violent, crime and drug-ridden ghetto.

My mother prayed to get out. She wanted desperately to move to a lovely individual home in a safe suburb. She fantasized about this, kept a folder of house plans and decorating ideas that she would peruse often. We were, I'm sure, one of the only families in our "hood" with a subscription to Southern Living Magazine. Later, when I was an adult, struggling myself, I would pick her up on weekends and we would visit model homes in new housing communities in the suburbs surrounding Baltimore. She prayed to, one day, own one of those homes herself.

As the years passed, my brother died, then my father, and my sister. I married and had children and my mother cared for my babies in that sagging row house in Baltimore. I divorced and bought my own home, but she would not move in with me. She helped me buy food and keep the lights on and buy toys for my children at Christmastime. And after caring for her dying family members for so many years, my mother went to work as a home health aide, caring for other dying people.

She was able to put together $1,500 and bought an acre of land in South Carolina near extended family members, and she planned to build a house on that land. Perhaps not the colonial she had once dreamed of. Maybe a small ranch home where she and Auntie and Unkie, her oldest sister and her husband could live.

But because of continuing financial struggle (perhaps from helping me and my children) my mother sold her acre of land. She was in her sixties and had had several heart attacks. The row home was crumbling around her and the neighborhood felt like a war zone, but she refused to sell the house and move to a senior citizens home, fearing the genetic disease would lay claim to one of her remaining children. She was determined to have a place where she could care for us if necessary. She also refused to move to Colorado to live with me when I later relocated, telling me she could not leave Auntie (fourteen years her senior) in Baltimore. I believe she still held out hope for her home in the suburbs. She had been in that "starter home" for forty years.

My mother never got her lovely home in the suburbs. A year before she died at age 70 from a final heart attack, she gave in and sold the decrepit row house, moving to the senior citizens home back over the bridge in the inner city where Auntie and Unkie lived. She had a miniscule one bedroom apartment down the hall from them. It was the most beautifully decorated apartment in the building.

In all her years of struggle and sacrifice, the only thing I recall my mother ever wanting was a nice house that she could decorate and live in with pride.

A year after my mother's death I built a home in a desirable area of Colorado Springs. Though it was not the first home I owned, or even the first one I had built, this was the first since my mother's death. When I moved into the others, my mother was still vibrant, her dream of owning her own lovely home in the suburbs still alive.

This time, as I walked through the door for the first time, I did not feel joy or excitement. I fell to the floor in my new home in the suburbs and wept for my mother.

BEARERS OF THE ARK

When the first living thing existed, I was there waiting.
When the last living thing dies, my job will be finished.
I'll put the chairs on the tables, turn out the lights
and lock the universe behind me when I leave.
∞ Neil Gaiman, *The Sandman, Vol. 3: Dream Country*

The thing that strikes me so poignantly about funerals is the men. There is something elegant and beautiful about Black men at funerals. They have looked on awkwardly as we women prepared the house and the food. Occasionally helpful in transporting chairs or lugging ice chests, their main job is to stay out of the way, to gather with other men in some adjacent area, and eat and reminisce. They are uncomfortable, powerless in the face of our grief.

But at the funeral, it is the men who reign.

In the end, they take their places with precision and bear the burden of our loved one's final earthly journey. At that moment, each man shouldering the casket—deacon and drug dealer, janitor and mechanic—is transformed. Even the most profane one becomes holy, sacred, a priest bearing the precious ark of the covenant to its resting place. I love these regal Black men then. Their solemn strength and dignity at each occasion of loss is reassuring to me. The cycle of life continues. Our women will continue to bring lives into the world, and at the appointed time, our men will silently carry them home.

BEEN DONE WRONG REVISITED

Breath by breath, let go of fear, expectation, anger, regret, cravings, frustration, fatigue. Let go of the need for approval. Let go of old judgments and opinions. Die to all that, and fly free. Soar in the freedom of desirelessness.
∞ Surya Das, *Awakening the Buddha Within*

It's been about two years since I wrote the blog, "Musings of a Mad Woman: *Been Done Wrong.*" In some ways, it feels like a lifetime. I feel like a different woman. I suppose that's what growth does for you. This journey is amazing.

Bit by bit, day by day, month by month, sometimes by leaps and bounds, more often at a frustratingly glacial pace, I am learning to let go. And I am so grateful for this journey. At first, I wondered if this was just a "time heals all wounds" type of process, but I don't think so. It is not just the passage of time, I am learning, but what you *do* in that time, how you *are* in that period that makes the difference.

I am not naïve about myself; I know my stuff. I acknowledge my weaknesses, flaws, hang-ups, and frailties and try (with varying levels of intensity) to work through them. Sometimes I stumble blindly in the process, in pain, crying out to God for relief. Often I seek help, searching out books and other resources to guide me. But looking back over these two years, I realize the one thing that has been most instrumental in my growth in this area has been the Power of Purpose.

I notice in that blog I wrote two years ago, I did not mention my mission. Over the last half year or so, I have focused on my personal mission with great intensity. I have determined to, not just have a beautifully written statement that I can point to with pride, but to actually live my mission, walk the talk. I worked to identify exactly what that mission statement meant to me, broke the statement down into actions and focused on implementing them in my life. When it became clear that the small non-profit where I worked could no longer afford my salary, I celebrated my layoff on the last day of 2011 as a beginning. I began my doctoral studies in January, became licensed to train using content from Laurie Beth Jones' *The Path* in March, and began my coaching and training business in April. Whew!

Furthermore, I began to align my thoughts, words and actions with my mission. When I focused on thoughts that were damaging to my esteem and spirit, I checked myself. When I behaved in ways that were counter to my purpose, I changed course, sought forgiveness, and moved forward. When I lashed out in anger or held on to old hurts, I asked myself, "Does this align with what you are about?" Decision by decision I began to shift my thoughts, words, and behavior. And the more I focused on what I was about, the more I let go of focusing on old wounds. And since I am literally a woman on a mission, I do not have the time or emotional space to nurture old hurts as I used to.

The more I realized and began to walk in who I am and how I am (based on my mission), the more I realized that I cannot manifest my highest self and my greatest potential while dragging old wounds and offenses around with me. They stifle my love, hinder my joy, and sabotage my success. And the more I realized I am filled with God's love, the more I wanted to be filled *only* with God's love. I want only to express love because that is who I am. So there is no place in me for old hurts. I forgive others to liberate myself to be only love. Only peace. Only Joy.

And this is not a one-time decision for me. I decide over and over again, at each opportunity to hold on to hurt, and each instance of feeling fear that letting *them* off the hook is allowing them to get away with disrespecting me or abusing me—I have to choose again each time that I am love and that my mission is to live a healed life; and to promote, inspire, and support the journey of inner healing and fulfilled purpose in others.

So I choose to let go, again and again. Until one day, I know this will not need to be a conscious choice. Who I am will just flow forth without thought or conscious intent. I am not perfect at this yet, but I'm on my way. I hope my daughter, now almost 26 years old, recognizes the change in me. Recognizes the value, imperative actually, of personal mission. And I hope she forgives me for being a mad woman. I love this journey.

Part II
I AM
∞
RE-MEMBERING

What I sought was not outside myself. It was within me, already there, waiting. Awakening was really the act of remembering myself ...
∞ Sue Monk Kidd, *The Dance of the Dissident Daughter: A Woman's Journey from Christian Tradition to the Sacred Feminine*

I AM EARTH

I am still learning—how to take joy in all the people I am, how to use all my selves in the service of what I believe, how to accept when I fail and rejoice when I succeed.
∞ Audre Lorde

Actually I am fire. And windy fire at that, as I have recently discovered. But I wanted to be earth.

Earth is strong, solid, foundational, and nurturing, consistent and persistent, capable and competent. I, on the other hand, was volatile. I was in my third marriage, and often on the edge of that one; I was often searching for something I could not name, never feeling I quite found my place. I was a temperamental, PMSy, fight or flight type of person (metaphorically speaking). Fiery. Windy. Me.

In Laurie Beth Jones's seminal work, *The Path*," she summarized a personality assessment she developed based on the four elements. Though she does not include the full assessment tool, she provides some guiding information to help determine the element that best aligns with one's personality. During my first reading of the book, I took a cursory stab at this section, knowing before I undertook the exercises that I am fire. But I wanted to be earth. During my recent second reading, I skipped that area of the book entirely, knowing that I am fire. But I wanted to be earth.

In Laurie Beth Jones' blog on her website, she also provided a brief introduction to the product. I tried every way to work it so that I could justify being earth, to no avail. I knew I was fire. Then a still, quiet voice said calmly within me, *"You **are** earth."* Huh? Vindication! I knew I was earth! Somewhere deep inside me was an earth hiding beneath the fire. Wasn't there?

I decided to put this question to the expert. I posted a comment on the blog seeking clarification from Laurie Beth herself. The source. Could you be one thing (fire) but feel in your gut that you should be another thing (earth)? Could you transform from one thing (fire) to another element (earth)? Could you be one element (fire), but God want you to be a different one (earth)? Or should I just accept my fiery self?

I received no answer to my queries and put the issue aside. Though I still wanted to be earth. About a week later I received the full assessment tool as part of my training to teach the concepts in *The Path*. Maybe I had somehow morphed from fire into earth in the couple of weeks since I had emailed Laurie Beth. I took the assessment and got the immediate results. Wind *and* fire. That was even worse. The total opposite of earth. Perhaps I misheard that still, small voice. Or maybe it was my ego speaking, substantiating my desire to be earth. Either way it was wrong, I am wind and fire.

My *Path* certification trainer was earth. She was calm and reasonable and logical. Man, I wanted to be earth. When we evaluated my assessment results we discussed the strong points and areas of opportunity of a wind/fire personality. I did have some earth elements, but I was very high wind and fire. Damn.

A week or so later, I went to the local Barnes & Noble to replace my lost copy of Ranier Maria Rilke's *Book of Hours: Love Poems to God*, my favorite volume of poetry. The store was out of copies. Incidentally, during that week, I had tuned into a PBS special featuring Dr. Wayne Dyer teaching his new book, *Wishes Fulfilled*. It was wonderful. I went to his website where he had a segment of a meditation tape that accompanied the book. The book and the tape were based on the Torah story of Moses and the burning bush and God's proclamation of His name—I Am that I Am. I began to meditate to that 20 minute audiotape segment each night as I fell asleep, reciting I AM affirmations for my life. A few days later, at the book store, unable to purchase my sought after volume of Rilke, I purchased instead the book, *Wishes Fulfilled*.

I began reading the book immediately and something on page 64 stopped me cold. Dyer, speaking of God indwelling each human being, reprinted lines of an Elizabeth Barrett Browning poem:

> *Earth's crammed with heaven,*
> *And every common bush afire with God;*
> *But only he who sees takes off his shoes,*
> *The rest sit round it and pluck blackberries.*

The next lines Dyer wrote were: "Yes, indeed, Earth's crammed with heaven, and *you are Earth*, filled to overflow with God. So take off your shoes and respect the holy space that is you."

There it was, *You are earth.* That still small voice was right. I am earth. And I am filled to overflow with God.

How amazing God is, and how amazing the ways he communicates with us. Jesus was fully man and fully God, wholly manifesting the nature of God in his life. Jesus was all that God is, and we, we are just as fully God as Jesus. He was the first begotten of God, not the only begotten. We are also God's children and, like Jesus, filled to overflow with God. The only difference is Jesus was operating at the highest (God) level of consciousness of this fact, and was fully living his God nature, miracles and all. We sit around picking berries for our existence, eschewing our God nature, unaware of the incredible Divine Power we are.

God has been speaking to me lately, reminding me that, like Jesus, I am fully Divine. It has been hard to wrap my windy/fiery mind around this, but I have been giving myself to this fact. I believe you, God, but help my unbelief, my resistance. Even putting aside the blasphemy of it all, how is it that this fiery/windy mad woman is fully God? Fully love? Don't I have to be meek and mild and flat and sort of ... vanilla? How can I be fully God and be Me?

The answer is... I don't know yet. Maybe I never will, maybe this is part of the mystery of life. Or maybe somewhere along this journey, the still small voice of God within me will whisper the answer. I just know I am fully God. And I now know I can only come from, act from, give from a place of love. There is no longer an option because that is who I am; there is nothing else in me. God is love. I am love. So in my fiery/wind way I will love like a mad woman, a holy woman, filled to overflow with God.

THE JOURNEY OF GENTLENESS

The greatest strength is gentleness.
∞ Native American Proverb, Iroquois

I am learning to be gentle. Quite a journey for this strong Black woman. I was gentle with babies and children, perhaps puppies. Adults were another matter. We should know better, we should get over it, we should toughen up and take control of ourselves and our situations. I was just as tough (or tougher) on myself. "Okay, Susan, stop whining and just get it done." (I can just hear Dr. Phil asking, "And how's that working out for you?")

And though, recognizing this about myself, I had begun to affirm "I am kind and caring and gentle" on a daily basis, I did not do so with the intention of treating myself in this manner. I wanted to think of and treat others with more kindness and gentleness.

Here's what I am coming to understand: though treating others this way is a laudable goal, it is not enough. To progress to the next phase of my journey, I must learn to extend this same gentle touch to myself. To speak to and handle myself with love. This is anathema to my tough, do what I need to do Black woman spirit, but necessary to my journey of becoming more fully who I am.

I am learning to be gentle with myself. Life can be challenging, and we, divine spirits on this human journey, often struggle to make our way. Instead of beating myself up for my frailties and beating back my fears, I am learning to honor this journey of growth. To be gentle with myself as I travel this path. Sometimes stumbling and crawling, every now and then dancing, once in a while soaring. Until that time when I soar more than stumble, celebrate more than commiserate, dance more than falter.

I love this journey. And I love myself.

HOW IS WHO SIDEWAYS

When I discover who I am, I'll be free.
∞ Ralph Ellison, *Invisible Man*

I struggled with God for many years, begging Him to show me HOW to be and HOW to do. HOW to act so people would like me, love me; HOW to have the life I wanted, HOW to live in peace.

I cannot say that God has given me lessons on how to be. And I no longer try to get people to like or love me. What I have learned over the years, however, is WHO I am. Life lesson: the "hows" always lead back to the who.

I was on one of my regular summer morning walks a few years ago. And I was lamenting the condition of my life; specifically my splintering relationship with my husband. There was always *stuff*. We needled each other, poking at open wounds, sniped constantly, argued frequently. I avoided his presence, leaving a room when he entered. It was miserable. I complained to God, "why is there no peace in the house? I just want peace." Hmmm … We had been in marriage counseling a few years earlier and the therapist asked us to write what we wanted from the marriage. My husband dutifully wrote his list. I wrote one word: Peace.

I just wanted peace. No poking. No sniping. No arguing. Just Peace. God answered me that morning on the trail in a way that I did not expect and did not particularly want to hear:

Why, God? Why is there no peace at home?

You don't have peace in your home because you do not bring peace to your home.

Excuse me?

If you do not have peace in your home it is because you do not bring peace to your home. You do not find *peace, Susan; you* bring *peace.*

ME? What about him? It takes two people to have peace you know.

If you don't have peace in your home it is because you do not bring peace to your home. What's the verse? You know the one I mean, you recite it all the time.

"Thou shalt keep him in perfect peace whose mind is stayed on thee, because he trusteth in thee."

Yes. Your peace is about you. And when you are in peace, you take peace wherever you go. You do not find peace, you bring peace.

But what about HIM?

That's between him and Me. You deal with you.

Damn! (Sorry, Lord). I did not like this lesson, but I understood it. And I tried to take peace with me, I really did. Sometimes successfully, sometimes not. This was a good first step, but a lesson further along the journey helped me begin to fully experience what God meant.

I am not sure there was a specific Ah Ha moment, but as I continued to seek and to study, I began to understand something that I always told my daughter. I had read the words somewhere and they resonated with me, but I did not yet fully understand their meaning or their power. When she would cry as a teenager, feeling she did not fit in, I would tell her, "My love, you are only responsible for becoming more fully who you are. And you are wonderful." She could not really get this at the time because she was just beginning to discover who she is. And I, even in my forties and fifties am just coming into the fullness of knowledge of who I am.

Here is what I am learning: I am in God and God in me. I am all that God is. God is peace so I am peace. I am not just IN peace. I AM peace. I no longer struggle to bring peace. Where ever I go there is peace because I AM peace. Only peace can flow from me because I am peace.

God is Love. I am love. I am not just loving, I AM love. There were times when I tried to love, as in do loving things. But when those things did not *work* (i.e. result in the sustained response I *expected*), I returned to my position of anger, resentment and insecurity. I don't struggle to love any more. I now know I AM love; only love can flow from me because love is who I am. Now my home is peaceful and I am in a loving, harmonious relationship with my husband. Knowing who I am and living who I am has made all the difference. The HOW I am flows from WHO I am.

Just turn your head a bit and look at the questions you ask from a different perspective. Not, how do I make money? But who am I in relationship to money? God is abundance. I am abundance. I know the money will manifest. I don't struggle with this anymore. I am prosperous, the money will flow. As I understand this, I live it more and more. I needed to order materials for my upcoming workshop. I did not quite have the money to do so and to do some other things I wanted to do. But it was okay, I am abundance, so I was not worried. I checked my account a few minutes ago, and the money I needed had come, right on time. I am abundance.

This does not mean that I sit passively and do nothing about my life. I had put into motion the thing that resulted in the deposit to my account, though I am never sure if and when the deposit will happen. I regularly *choose* to love, because I know I am love. I remind myself that I have no options: I am love so I do love. I am not passive. I work on my business, work on my relationship, work to make my dreams come true. But now it is with an air of inevitability, not some pipe dream I struggle with. I am all that God is, and God is not a failure. This does not mean that I will not have missteps and screw-ups from time to time. But I know I am destined to win in the long run. Because of who I am.

The HOW of your life flows from the WHO. Once you know and live WHO you are, HOW you think, speak, and behave will just begin to flow and you will attract what you are. The key is not doing; the key is being. Be love, and you will love and you will attract love. Be peace, and you will create peace. Be prosperous and what you need will flow. This lesson has transformed my life. I love this journey.

THE JOURNEY TO RE-MEMBER AND RE-MIND

It is terrible how much has been forgotten, which is why,
I suppose, remembering seems a holy thing.
∞ Anita Diamant, *The Red Tent*

Life can bestow such incredible gifts. Like grandchildren. I am in love.

My grandson called me yesterday. "Hi Grandma. I haven't heard from you in a while so I thought I would call and check on you." Wow! "I miss you so very, very much, Grandma. I think about you all the time. I even dream about you. I can even see your face in my mind." Wow again!

Six years old, my grandson is brilliant and beautiful and loving and incredibly charming and full of energy and excitement. This child is amazing, and he is part of me, has my blood flowing in his veins. What a legacy to leave—

another generation of life, another answer to the pain and suffering in the world.

At six years old, this young mind is so full of promise; he can become whatever in the world he wants. A few months ago, it was a doctor, then an astronaut, then a deep sea diver. At six years old, however, he also believes what he is told about himself. And I pray (though experience tells me otherwise) that what he is told will not conflict with and interfere with what he knows intuitively about himself—that he is a unique expression of God in the earth. That he has come from God and carries God within himself; that he is all God is. That he is infinite possibility.

The older we grow, the more prone we are to forget this. Or more accurately, the more the voices and experiences around us drown out the voice and experience of God within us and we find ourselves limited only to what we believe we can be and do.

Thankfully, however, another incredible gift we have been given is that of re-membering and re-minding. We have the ability to re-member and re-mind ourselves of who we really are. To re-member this is to intentionally reassemble from the scattered places in our hearts and brains, who we were before we became indoctrinated (however lovingly) into who we think we are.

To *mind* (verb) is to attend to, be conscious of, take care of. When we re-mind ourselves of who we really are, we focus our attention once again on our true nature. And we take care of, nurture this knowing, until it again becomes our continuous conscious reality. Until we know that we, no matter our age or station in life, are infinite possibility. And that we can become whatever we want.

"Yeah, sure," you say doubtfully. "What if I want to be a prima ballerina"?

Do you want to be a prima ballerina?

"Well, no, but what if I wanted to be one. I am 50 years old. I can't be a prima ballerina."

Well, that's no problem, since you don't want to be one. You can be whatever you WANT to be.

Why do we argue that we cannot be whatever we want because there are things we cannot be? And why do we focus on what we cannot be when that's not what we want to be anyway? Human nature? Hmmm … Perhaps if we acted from our God nature, we would know for sure that we are infinite possibility and whatever we desire in alignment with our purpose, we can fulfill.

The issue is that we have forty-five (or however many) years of human voices and experiences filling our minds with our limitations.

It is time to re-mind ourselves about who we really are. And here's the key. Re-minding is not a one-time activity. We have many, many years of thinking to undo. Those limiting beliefs will return again and again; that's what they have been trained to do. We must act just as tenaciously in replacing them with affirmations of our true nature—over and over again, thought by thought. If we give up on this, we resign ourselves to life within the realm of our illusions, our limitations.

For some people that's okay. Frankly, God gives us permission to do just that if that is what we desire.

As for me, there are certainly times when I give in to the illusions of my limitations. There are moments when I forget who I am. Before, it would take me years or months or weeks to recover from these lapses. But now, I am happy to report, within a day or two I re-member who I am, take a deep breath and begin living infinite possibility again.

My grandson says he wants to be like me; he wants to go to college and be very smart. He does not know that I want to be like him—intuitively knowing with absolute certainty that I am infinite possibility and I can be whatever I want. And like him, I want to continuously live my life from this position of divine wonder. What a journey!

WOMEN'S WORK

*The way black women say "girl" can be magical.
Frankly, I have no solid beliefs about the survival of consciousness
after physical death. But if it's going to happen I know what
I want to see after my trek toward the light.
I want to see a black woman who will smile and say, "Girl...."*
∞ Abigail Padgett, *Blue*

Yesterday I caught my first fish, a rainbow trout about 12 inches long. He (or she) was beautiful. My first fishing expedition was an outing with the girls—five beautiful Black women over fifty—at a stocked lake in "the community" in Colorado Springs. We joked and teased, caught up on the latest news, and flirted a little with the brothers who stopped by occasionally to give us advice (of course).

The three of us who were novices came in full makeup, one sporting gold hoop earrings and a gold chain (You know who you are). We were pretty lousy fisherman. We cast our lines into each other's lines, into the muddy bank, and once, onto the railing separating us from the lake. We caught just that one fish between the three of us. Many earthworms gave their lives in vain that day, but we sure looked good and we enjoyed each other's company.

There is something incredibly beautiful about grown up Black women — wise, intelligent, lively, caring, and supportive, sometimes outrageous. There is nothing like a woman's love and strength and beauty. When we are confident about ourselves, knowing and secure in who we are, we are a formidable force. We can ignite love in hardened hearts, feed the earth's children, transform communities, and change the world.

When we forget who we are, however, we can give into the illusion that the "other" is the enemy, and become a dangerous foe, some woman's worst nightmare, a blight on our communities. When we lose sight of our divine nature and abilities, and forget we are love, we add to the world's suffering.

Here's what I am learning. We are all one. The wiser I become, the more I realize that separation is only an illusion. We are inextricably linked in a beautiful web of life. When we hurt one, we hurt ourselves. I will no longer allow petty differences, or perceived major ones, to separate me (even in an illusory fashion) from my sisters. From my sisters here and all over the globe. We are the answer to the world's fear and pain and suffering.

We caught one fish yesterday, but that was enough. A woman can take one fish and create a stew that feeds the entire neighborhood.

The essence of this journey is in coming to know, and then realigning ourselves with, who we really are. And then healing a hurting world. This is women's work.

WHAT IF...

I AM
Programmed to forget
Who I am...
My brothers are wandering in the wilderness of confusion
And I am lost among them...
∞ Jerome Jones and Mo Beasley, *No Good Nigga@ BlueZ*

A few nights ago, I did not remember I am love. I bought into the illusion that I had to verbally fight—to be mean, combative, hurtful. That I had an enemy in the form of another person who (at that moment) radiated hatred toward me. If I were a woman easily intimidated I would have retreated—and wisely so. But since I am not that woman, either easily intimidated or always wise, I matched their loathing with my own. Eyes narrowed, I spat the words, "I hate you."

I am ashamed. This is me, a grown up Black woman, Love incarnate. The woman who affirms to myself each and every day, at least once a day that I am love. Yet when pushed, challenged, I quickly forgot who I am and morphed into that person who used to look like me, that mad woman wearing my clothes.

What is really going on when we think or speak or behave in ways not aligned with our authentic selves?

As I recall, my forgetting who I am was not so quick as I first believed. Frankly, I was in a phase of self-doubt during the time of this awful confrontation. I was struggling to believe who I am in different areas of my life. These doubts manifested in various "benign" ways—in a business letter I wrote that did not exude self-confidence, in hesitating to move forward in certain areas of my life. But more significantly, that self-doubt, unattended, subconsciously extended to the belief that I am love. And perhaps, because I felt insecure in myself, in who I really am, and therefore of what I am capable, I projected that self-loathing on the other person, charging them as an imposter also, and both inciting and mirroring their rage. This disturbing incident was the culmination of weeks of self-doubt and fear. Within, I had been struggling, "What if I am not who I think I am"?

We are most dangerous when we are insecure about our true nature and capabilities. Our world becomes a reflection of our fear. We doubt our divine aspects and abilities and are perched perilously between the authentic world (a world in which we are conscious of, and experience our world from the vantage point of who we really are) and a world created by our self-imposed illusions of fear and failure and scarcity and separation. The "other" becomes our enemy, when there really is no other. Wars are fought because of this, and acts of terror and retaliation committed. Our fight or flight instinct is triggered. But the danger is not real; it is just our illusion. We doubt, or perhaps do not remember, who we are.

Here's the lesson: when we leave our self-doubts and fears unattended, we become predators—our own worst enemies, and enemies of those in our orbit. We live out our fears in relationship with ourselves and with others.

We know what it is like to have a partner or loved one who is insecure and seeks to control others. Who is unhappy with him or herself so is spiteful or jealous or perpetually angry or continually in crisis and drama. And most of us have been this person at one time or another.

When self-doubt and limiting beliefs creep in, acknowledge them and deal with them right away. If you do not, you will continue to have issues with self-love and problems in relationships with others.

Every human being experiences moments of self-doubt. The key is to handle those feelings before they invade all areas of your life. Become critically self-reflective so you know when those self-doubts begin to arise. Then do not allow yourself to languish in your fear. Do something. Seek someone who can help you reaffirm who you are. Get away if you can and do self-work. Read the book that re-charges you. Gather your tribe around you to help you; not those who just comfort you where you are, but those who can help you see and believe who you really are. And pray. And meditate. Do something.

Your success and your joy and the quality of your relationships depend on you knowing and living who you are. Do not allow doubt and fear and limiting beliefs to become or continue to be the obstacles that stop you from fulfilling your dreams and your purpose in the earth. Lack, fear, scarcity, enemies—all are illusions that, if you believe them, will relegate you to a lesser life. You are magnificent and abundance and love and perfect peace and joy and fulfilled and whatever else is in alignment with God's best for you. Deal with your doubts and enjoy the journey!

A CONVERSATION WITH GOD— RELAX

To have faith is to trust yourself to the water. When you swim you don't grab hold of the water, because if you do you will sink and drown. Instead you relax, and float.
∞ Alan Wilson Watts

Sometimes trusting God seems so difficult. I think I am fully trusting, but then an issue arises. I immediately whisper, "I trust you, God." But my body tells me differently. A headache begins to build, my stomach feels queasy, and my bowels break down. All physical manifestations of stress. My dis-ease tells me I am not trusting God, am not in perfect peace. But I am trying, I really am. I know God has never failed me. I know I will be okay however the issue turns out. I know this. But in some way, I am holding on to the problem, trying to work it out myself. But aren't I supposed to actively seek solutions? Is trusting God just passively waiting for

Him/Her to move? Obviously I'm doing this trusting thing all wrong.

As I reflect, mainly money issues cause this dis-ease in me. This has been the case as long as I can remember. Growing up poor in Baltimore, money was always a problem. When raising my children, I would get migraines on Saturdays when I handled the bills. There never seemed to be enough money. And I often felt guilty that I did not effectively manage the money we had. I was afraid I made a wrong decision, screwed up in some way that caused us major financial pain. I was always afraid, not trusting myself to make the right decisions. Afraid I was not capable of handling such a grown up task; afraid that I was putting my family in jeopardy.

I still feel this today. Literally today. I made a decision I thought was a good one for me and my business. But as I added up costs in my head, the dis-ease began to rise up in me. I recited, "I trust you, God." Then my daughter called and asked for help paying her rent. I said, "I trust you, God." The headache began to pound in my temples. I felt a sick, woozy feeling in my stomach. I rushed to the bathroom as the diarrhea surprised me. Dis-ease. Now I sit propped up in my bed trying to figure out where I am going wrong in my journey of trusting God.

Stress in my life manifests in physical woes; for many years headaches, often the migraine variety. Now I don't get the painful migraines very often, just stress headaches and major stomach woes, immediate diarrhea and the nausea that accompanies migraines, though without the intense head pain. I get mainly painless migraines now. This dis-ease tells me my body and mind and emotions are out of balance in some way. It tells me I am not in the perfect peace which comes from trusting God.

So *how* do I trust you, God? What are the mechanics of doing so? What do I think, what do I say, how do I *do* it? I want to know, to grow in this area. I want to trust you. I hate this stress, this pain. Help me.

Relax, God tells me.

RELAX?

You are making it too hard. Just relax and let the answer flow. It's okay. The answer will come. You do not need to work so hard at it. Just relax and let the answer flow.

But don't I have to *do* something?

Relax. Here's the answer for today's situation:

Just tell the truth. "I miscalculated and I must push this off until the following Wednesday." You made a mistake. It is okay. Forget about trying to save face. If she is the person you are to work with then she will understand. Relax. Stop beating yourself up. Just relax and let the answer flow. Relax knowing the answer will come.

You could have told me this before I crapped in my pants.

You were too busy to listen.

Relaxing does not come naturally or easily to me. I am a fire/wind personality. Intense, sometimes high strung, anxious, type A. I can tell others that God will take care of *it*. But for me? I typically want a formula. I want to know the mechanics of it. What to think, what to say, what to do. In other words, I want to be in control. Relaxing is doing nothing. Isn't it?

No, relaxing is trusting, relaxing is letting go of control. Relaxing is allowing your body and your emotions, your heart to become aligned with what you know. That it will be okay. Just relax. Be still for a few moments—emotionally, mentally, and intellectually. Allow the answer to flow. Relax

Why is it that the most profound truths, the most transformative solutions are so simple?

God, I love this journey. God, I love you.

WHAT I KNOW TO DO

The journey of a thousand miles begins with a single step.
∞ Lao Tzu

*I*f only I could see the whole picture; a panoramic view of answers and solutions laid out before me. How to make your business grow into your ideal vision? Okay, here's step one, then step two, now step three … walk right this way. How to manifest your highest self? Well, first you do this, then that, then … don't you see it? The path ends right over there and voila!

I could get into that.

But for this sister (and for most of us, I suspect), life does not unfold like a mural with yellow bricks I can see stretching into the distance, guiding me along an illuminated ochre path. I was sure, at one point in my life, that that plan must be reserved for wholesome White girls from the heartland with wide-eyed innocence and overactive imaginations. My White friends, however, have disabused me of that notion.

Me, I squint and strain and stress, trying to see the WAY. I am sure the path is there somewhere, but often the climate of my life, and perhaps my own astigmatic vision, obscures all but the very next brick. Sometimes my world is so stormy and foggy, or dark, or so bright that I feel blinded. And frequently, the next brick is not a step away, but a leap forward, and I must launch myself into the uncertain air to reach it.

I am fifty four years old, and frankly, this walking by faith and not by sight stuff is getting a little old.

Come on God, give a sister a break.

Don't worry about the whole journey; I've got that. Just take the next step.

But it's way over there!

Yep.

Can't you make it easier to reach? A little less scary?

Nope. I've told you what to do. Just take the next step.

But then what?

Just do what you know to do. You'll know what's next when the time is right.

But …

Do what you know to do.

What a transformative lesson this has been for me. And not one I always embrace. Here's the key:

You know what to do next. Do it.

You *know* what to do. And this does not mean necessarily doing what you've done in the past. Your intuition, that still small voice, something you have recently learned, or your common sense has spoken to you. It is often not a huge or complex task, but sometimes it does require courage. And you don't have to see the whole picture. In fact, you rarely see the whole picture. Just do what you know to do.

I have often resisted this. What I know to do sometimes seems scary or overwhelming or, frankly, so trite or insignificant. Make the phone call, or send the email, or write the letter, or read the information, or prepare the lesson. Just do it. This is so simple, but sometimes so difficult to execute. I hesitate or procrastinate or avoid, afraid, or not seeing the reason for doing it, or … And I am left standing on the same brick, immobile, until I simply do what I know to do. Then, without fail, the next step appears, the next thing I need to know comes to me, the connection bears fruit.

Sometimes we make the journey so complex. And often, like me, we want to see the whole picture, to know the complete plan, to control the entire process. When all we need to do is take the next step. All that is required of us this moment is to do what we know to do, and trust the next step will be revealed to us.

In order to get unstuck, to move forward, take a lesson from a grown up Black woman. Do what you know to do.

THE WORLD OF OTHER PEOPLE

Of course I'll hurt you. Of course you'll hurt me. Of course we will hurt each other. But this is the very condition of existence. To become spring, means accepting the risk of winter. To become presence, means accepting the risk of absence.
∞ Antoine de Saint-Exupéry, The Little Prince

*I*t's not fair.
Life is moving along smoothly. You are in your groove swing, doing your thing, feeling content. You are prayed up, walking your talk and everyone is impressed.

And then, seemingly out of nowhere, the crap hits the fan, often in the form of relationship drama. Significant other, family, friends, colleagues—something gets someone out of whack and you are embroiled in conflict and grief and aggravation and pain.

I think it was Jean Paul Sartre who said "hell is other people." Today I am inclined to agree.

Today, I would like to be on an island, just writing and affirming and communing with God, being grateful in blissful solitude. On my island, when I tire of writing, I put on a smooth tune, maybe Teddy or Luther or Maysa. On my island life is perfect, and I am perfect. I am perfect love, perfect peace, perfect joy.

Damn, I would even settle for remaining in my sanctuary; that room in our home that is just mine. There I am surrounded by the things I love. I can close the door and ignore the phone, and just BE. I love the stillness of my space; it is heaven.

But eventually, I must venture out into the world; the world of other people. Where crap happens. Where feelings get hurt, boundaries are breached, and insecurity reigns. Where people make me crazy and I rub them the wrong way. Where I screw up. Where there is jealousy and fear and pain. Where I forget I am love and rage like a madwoman. Where I believe the illusion that there is "the other" and that I must "win." Where I say the wrong thing. Where I misunderstand and am misunderstood. Where I get hurt and hurt those I love.

After being in the world with other people for a while, I cannot wait to return to my peaceful, solitary sanctuary. But here's what I am learning: Life is about relationships, and we learn life's lessons as we relate to those with whom we interact on this journey.

Without our fellow travelers we cannot grow or mature or become fully who we are. It is in relationship with those on our path that we act out the personal enlightenment we seek in our times of solitude, prayer or meditation. Patience, love, peace, joy, unity. In solitude we seek these gifts and they are freely given to us, but they are perfected as we relate with others.

It is easy to be love when it's just me and God; it is easy to experience joy or peace. But in relationships, our "stuff" comes up. And it is only when our weaknesses and flaws and fears rise to the surface, that they can be healed. That we can advance toward fully becoming who we are.

Life is acted out in relationship with others. There are times that we go to our quiet space and recharge and renew and commune in a special way with God. These times are as necessary for me as air and water. But these are the in-between times; we are not meant to live our lives here. Our relationship with God and our relationship with ourselves are lived out as we commune with others. That's where the mirror is held up to us. That's where we really express who we are.

I am in my sanctuary again, renewing myself. Soon I will step out, once more, into the world of other people. And this time, I will be stronger, more firmly rooted in who I am. This time I will remember I am love and will walk in the perfect peace that I am. This time, I will have grown.

The Bible tells us to pray without ceasing; not just in our solitary "prayer time." Everything we do is prayer. Relationship with others is certainly prayer; a sweet incense raised to God. Each smile is praise; each loving deed, salvation; each act of forgiveness, halleluiah. This, I am learning, is the essence of the journey.

THE THING ABOUT TUNNELS

The cave you fear to enter holds the treasure you seek.
∞ Joseph Campbell

The thing about tunnels is they are usually dark and somewhat scary places. Our fears scurry in tunnels avoiding the light of open spaces; our doubts whisper to us from tunnel walls. But tunnels are often the quickest way, sometimes the only way, to get from where we are to our next destination on the journey.

The Pros and Cons of Tunnels:
Pro: Tunnels are great hiding places if you think your opponent is above or outside.
Con: Not so good if your fears reside within you.
Pro: Tunnels can be effective shelters from storms.
Con: Not so much if the storm is in your own mind or heart.
Pro: Tunnels get you from here to there faster.
Con: Tunnels are scary as hell.

Pro: Tunnels can be cool residences if you are homeless or a vampire.

Con: See Con above (except if you're a vampire in which case *you* are as scary as the tunnel). And tunnels were not designed for living.

I have been through many tunnels.

The tunnels of our lives are those frightening stretches of the path we must traverse to continue to our destination. They often represent a lesson or a fear or a challenge that we must get through in order to continue our growth. Sometimes tunnels represent those disorienting stretches of the journey between here and there. No longer here, but not quite there. Those dark spaces between phases, where what we did before no longer works, but where we have not yet acquired the knowledge or skills for where we are going. We are awkward in the tunnels of our lives, blindly fumbling to grasp and articulate that which we do not yet understand.

I have been known to stand quaking at a tunnel entrance, peering in fearfully, immobile for days or weeks or years. I know I must enter or I will remain stalled, unable to reach the next phase of my life. So eventually I have stepped tentatively in, swiping at unseen forces, avoiding the temptation to return to the safety of the light I can still see behind me. And then that light disappears. And I drop to my knees, crying and crawling through some areas, groping and grasping. My mind tells me to go back; that I will die in this darkness, that I am not strong enough to make it through. Or to shut down, to roll myself into a protective ball, knees to chest, and wait to be rescued. But something stronger than my mind keeps me moving forward, sometimes sobbing and raging, but slowly advancing until I see a dim light ahead. And each time I do this, that light feels like salvation.

At this point in my journey, I know by experience that I can survive the tunnels of my life. That when I emerge from the other end, I will have grown wiser, and stronger, and more fully who I am. That I am then able to meet the challenges and embrace the opportunities in the next phase of my life. And I have learned that being "saved" is a not one-time event, but that at the end of each tunnel, at every inch of growth, at each victory, at each movement along this journey—Salvation!

THE VOICES IN MY HEAD

These pains you feel are messengers. Listen to them.
∞ Rumi

You have no idea what you are doing, my mind whispers. Step back, this will only cause you pain, my body intones, as a headache builds in my temples. *You are going to screw up. You will fail in front of everyone. They already know you don't follow through. Don't embarrass yourself.*

I am changing the way I deal with limiting thoughts. Until very recently, I believed the way to handle my self-doubts and limiting beliefs was to counteract and override them with affirmations of my highest self. If I could outlast the beliefs by talking louder and more persistently, I could eventually push them away permanently. Sometimes I would give these negative thoughts a stern, angry, commanding "Get behind me, Satan!" in true Christian form. But generally, I tried to push these thoughts away, believing that attending to these fears gave them power in my life.

I was only partially right.

I am learning to allow these doubts and limiting beliefs to speak to me. Reluctantly, and contrary to my beliefs and practices, I have begun to give them voice, to listen to their concerns. When my body is in dis-ease because of fear, I have begun to allow it to tell me why it is afraid. When the self-doubts arise or my fears caution me to retreat, I now hear them out.

You don't have the money, or the intelligence, or the willpower to make this work. You know you will give up eventually, why not save yourself time and money and energy. It's scary over there; stay here where it is safe. You're just lying to yourself, you haven't really changed. You never finish anything. You are a loser. What makes you think this time will be different?

I am learning that, no matter how negative the message, our minds really just want to keep us safe. When we want to launch out into uncharted (for us) waters, our minds want to pull us back to the safety of familiar shores where we are not in danger or in pain. Our minds tell us whatever they can to keep us safe.

The problem is we, our minds, have been indoctrinated through our relationships and other life experiences about what is "safe." Having lots of money will make you evil, we may have learned, so our minds tell us we should only earn so much and no more.

Trying new things is scary. Don't go to college, you might fail and that would be painful. Stay here because your friends are here and they make you feel good. Go to college, but major in accounting because you can get a good job and take care of your future family. Being an entrepreneur is hard and takes lots of money and people may not support you. The office is what you know and what earns you a decent living so do not try to be an artist.

Our minds try to limit us to what we, through our life experiences, have been taught is best (safest) for us, even though these limitations may not align with what we now want for ourselves. This is really a form of love, though it is love misaligned. These "dangers" are only illusions, but our minds don't know that. Our minds are only trying to keep us safe.

And I am learning to stop battling my mind and to honor this desire for my wellbeing. So I now listen to the limiting thoughts in my mind, the fears that manifest in my body. And I respond to them. I thank my mind for wanting to keep me safe, and I gently tell it (myself) that it is okay. That I don't know everything about my new venture, but I am learning, and I continue to be divinely connected with those who can help me along the way. And I tell my mind, myself, that God is with me, in me, and He/She has this. So it is okay, let's relax, we can do this. It is okay to be scared, but I can handle it.

I no longer try to ignore or overpower or fight my fears, limiting thoughts, and self-doubts. They are not the enemy; they are very much a part of this journey of growth. I give them voice and attend to them, but not in a way that empowers them. I address them (myself) with love and kindness and gentleness, all the while continuing to affirm my highest self. And I move forward, not by beating myself and my thoughts back, but by honoring myself and my mind's desire to keep me safe along this very human journey of fulfilled purpose.

And this is making all the difference.

THE POWER OF PURPOSE

She had not known the weight until she felt the freedom.
∞ Nathaniel Hawthorne, *The Scarlet Letter*

We know intellectually that holding on to old pain and hurts limits our ability to move forward in our lives. We cannot manifest our highest selves and our greatest potential while dragging old wounds and offenses around with us. They stifle our love and creativity, hinder our joy, and sabotage our success. We know this. But the question I hear a lot and see people asking on television talk shows and in conferences is "*how* do I let go?" How do I actually *do* it? I am almost always disappointed in the answer these seekers are given; usually just a replay of the necessity to liberate yourself so that you can move forward in your life. That is certainly true, but *how* to do it, well that's another matter.

Today, I am going to give you the bottom line on the HOW of letting go of old pain caused by others or just by life circumstances. As with most transformative solutions, it is not complex and it does not cost hundreds or thousands of dollars. It is not particularly sexy. It is simple, elegant, though not necessarily easy or an immediate fix.

Here is how you let go:
One decision at a time. One thought at a time.

In the past, I would ruminate on old hurts, sometimes for extended periods of time, and often in situations where I was conducting mindless activities. Cooking or dusting or standing in front of the mirror perming and styling my hair or putting on makeup. I would roll the old hurtful event around in my mind, fantasying about the different responses I would make to the perpetrator. I would conjure up new situations where the offender would show his/her stripes in front of witnesses, and I, having been publicly wounded, would be vindicated by the fact that others now know the type of person he/she really is, and will understand what I have endured all of this time. Poor me. My mind would re-play these scenarios at every opportunity, seemingly at will. This was such a comforting and comfortable activity for me, that it would be several minutes before I even realized I was doing it.

This continual contemplation of and focus on the hurt, of course, only served to keep me locked in its embrace. But it felt so comfortable being the victim, I could not even imagine how it would feel to be free. I knew this was not emotionally healthy, but it felt so good. This old hurt was a familiar lover and, after all, "the devil you know is better than the devil you don't." I was comfortable with this feeling, this sensation. If I let it go, what would replace it? Totally illogical, I know, but that was my mindset.

Now, however, since I have begun to walk in my purpose, I am critically conscious of the thoughts in my head and I challenge them. I recognize earlier and earlier that I am in the midst of debilitating ruminations and I make a conscious choice to change my thoughts to those in alignment with my mission. When I first began practicing this, I had to make that decision every few minutes as I would find myself returning to the negativity over and over again, almost subconsciously. My self-rebuke would last only seconds and I was submerged once again in the thoughts. I would stop myself again, only to find myself back minutes later. Over and over again, I would make the decision to change my thoughts until my brain finally began to get with the program. I found myself going "there" less and less, and I realized earlier and earlier in the process that I was there. And the change began lasting longer and longer. One decision at a time, one thought at a time, I was letting go.

And since I had been afraid on some level of what my mind would do if I no longer had those negative thoughts to comfort me, I created new thoughts aligned with my purpose. "I am love. I am perfect peace. I am forgiving. I am victorious. I am living a healed life. I am joy!" I replaced those "victim" thoughts with thoughts of victory—with visions of who I really am, guided by my purpose, which is aligned with God's best for me. I am letting go, decision by decision. Each time those negative thoughts show up, I choose to let go of them. I choose to replace them with affirmations of my highest self. This is how you let go. One decision at a time. This is the power of purpose.

Try these helpful tips to align your thoughts with your purpose and let go of old wounds:

1. Create and write a list of new thoughts—affirmations aligned with your purpose and who you now know yourself to be..

2. View each opportunity to replay old thoughts as an opportunity to change, to grow into who you really are.

3. When you find yourself focusing on old hurts, say "I choose a new thought," and recite an affirmation. i.e. "I choose a new thought; I am love." Continue to repeat that new thought until it takes root in your mind and replaces the negative one. Do this each time you find yourself mired in negative thinking.

4. Recite your affirmations to yourself daily. It is especially helpful to do this as you fall asleep, so these thoughts are embedded in your consciousness.

5. Keep your mission statement, your statement of purpose before you. Remind yourself often of who you are and why you were put on the earth.

What a wonderful feeling when you realize you are growing into who you are. This is the power of purpose.

Enjoy the journey!

THE JOURNEY OF STILLNESS

Begin by being still. Quiet the outer world, so that the inner world might bring you sight.
∞ Neale Donald Walsch

I love stillness. In stillness, God holds my hand. In stillness, I am so fulfilled tears well in my eyes. In stillness, I am inseparable from God.

I have learned to be still.

In earlier years, I was in perpetual motion. A sister on the rise; afraid of the silence. Afraid if I were still, I would have to come face to face with myself, and that I would not like the person I thought I was.

I did have that inevitable meeting one fateful day. And that day I began the journey of becoming who I am.

And now I treasure the stillness. In stillness I honor God-in-me.

There is a season for all things; for motion and for stillness. In motion, I live out what I cultivate in stillness.

That I am Love. I am perfect peace. I am unlimited potential. I am joy. I am one with God.

I love stillness. I love this journey.

I AM THAT I AM

Relationships do not cause pain and unhappiness.
They bring out the pain and unhappiness that is already in you.
∞ Eckhart Tolle

I am that I am. Except when I forget. Yesterday I forgot I am love. I forgot I am loving acceptance and loving agreement and entered into a drawn out verbal battle with someone I love dearly. I fought valiantly for my stand about a hypothetical situation that may happen years from now, or never. What insanity! When I hung up the phone in the wee hours of the morning, feeling smug that I had "won," my spirit gently re-minded me who I am. And I nearly wept in shame. I begged God's forgiveness, then texted my loved one apologizing for my temporary lapse in sanity. Then I forgave myself and transitioned slowly into sleep.

Here is what I know: It is never about the other person or about the situation or the issue. It is always, always,

always about ME (about you). It doesn't matter what SHE said or HE did. It matters not if they are "wrong" or "right." The situation is of no consequence. The only thing that matters is ME. Who I am being in response to that situation; in relationship to that person. And I was not being who I am. Because I am love; I am loving acceptance and loving agreement, I am harmony and unity and oneness, I am perfect peace. But just for a moment (actually a couple hours), I forgot that. I bought into the illusion that there is an *other* and that I was on the opposite side of an issue and that I had to be *right*. In truth, there is no *other*. I am one with all of life; we are all one. When I battle with someone else, I am really fighting myself, dishonoring myself, destroying my own peace and well-being.

I am so grateful that God, the universe, my own spirit constantly re-mind me who I am. My role is to BE; to express who I am, who I choose to be in every situation. To BE love, and light, and joy, and hope and help, and patience and persistence, and fulfilled, and compassionate and kind and caring and gentle, and forgiving, and perfect peace, and harmony and unity and oneness, and abundance and prosperous, and a blessing, and divine perfect health. And to demonstrate this being-ness in *every* experience of my life. This I know.

Life provides and my soul draws, over and over again, opportunities for me to demonstrate who I am. And in those dark moments when I forget, and act like the mad woman I used to be, God causes me to re-member, to literally pull myself together once more from my illusion of separation and fragmentation. To become, in effect, whole again; divinely knowing the truth of oneness with Him and all of life. Then I forgive myself, create myself anew, and once again, I am that I am.

MCDONALDS AND ME—BILLIONS AND BILLIONS SERVED

Love is a selfless service to mankind like a showcase done by the twinkling stars in the beautiful nightly sky.
∞ Santosh Kalwar

Recently, I've felt like I am doing the right things for the wrong reasons.

I have worked diligently for the last few weeks to increase traffic to my social media sites and the blog they support. And my efforts have borne fruit, proving that dedication and hard work pay off. My Facebook page "likes" have quadrupled, and my blog views and Twitter followers have dramatically increased. This has been very time-intensive work, requiring hours online a day and causing me to neglect other priorities in my life. I have been assessing each of my sites numerous times daily to check my progress.

But in my heart, an unease has begun to take root. I also need to check myself. What is really my motive for this focused, almost obsessive, activity? Is it to build support so publishers will more readily accept my book, so that I can inspire more people with my story? Is it to promote, inspire, and support the journey of inner healing and fulfilled purpose in others? Or is it to assuage my ego? I am delighted when I see the count rising on my blog. Each new "like" on my Facebook page makes me happy. Has this become about me?

Dr. Wayne Dyer describes ego as **E**dging **G**od **O**ut. Is that what I am doing? Am I increasing my reach in love for the people I may impact? Or, like McDonalds, am I just feeding my ego by counting those who have clicked the "follow" or "like" button? 34 served. 395 served. 800 served.

We are taught in college and in industry that we must find ways to measure our success. How do we know the extent to which we are meeting our goals, or whether what we are doing is working unless we count? And we think that *count* matters. In fact, we insist that *count* matters, as we judge our success based on those numbers. We fire those who cannot deliver the numbers, and bring in new talent who will. No wonder people cheat—pad the books, inflate the numbers, lie about the test scores.

Here's what I am learning: Without true love and caring for those we reach, our increased "numbers served" only reflects "the insane notion of counting noses" as Socrates put it. Our work becomes about our ego, not about transforming lives or meeting the nutritional needs of a bloated population. And one day we look up from our counting and notice we have become predators, doing whatever it takes to increase the numbers.

Well, I choose to change this paradigm in my life. Now. Though I have affirmed each night, "I touch millions of people with my work," I now add, "because we are One and I love them and desire their greatest good." And I mean it. My journey is not only about my healed life, though it began there; it is about a healed world. And a Love so deep and divine that it transforms lives. It is not me, or even my message, but the Love that undergirds me and my message, that transforms lives.

I will continue to work to expand my message's reach, but now with the intention of loving each one reached. It is not about the numbers, but about love. God is love and I am love. And I will love each one like a mad woman, a holy woman, filled to overflow with Love. Filled to overflow with God.

I am so grateful for this journey.

Part III

I AM
∞
HOME

I have arrived. I am home. My destination is in each step.
∞ Thich Nhat Hahn

TOMORROW

Tomorrow. The word hangs in the air for a moment, both a promise and a threat ...
∞ Thrity Umrigar, *The Space Between Us*

It is 4:05 in the morning, and I am terrified.

I switch on the bedside lamp and lift my laptop onto my knees. I want to describe this experience, I want to understand it, I want to heal it.

I have been having trouble sleeping for weeks. I twist and turn for hours, on the edge of consciousness, not really asleep, but not fully awake. And in this not-quite state, I dream. In the dreams I am scared, terrified. I guess they are more like nightmares. I had several of these dreams tonight, or this morning as the case is. I gasp for breath coming out of each one. I get up and go to the bathroom to fully disengage. I have done this three times tonight. And now, finally, I turn on the light, and pull out my laptop and struggle to describe this, to understand what is going on, to re-member.

These are not the something-is-chasing-me dreams I had in my early years, or the I-can't-quite-get-there dreams or the I-search-and-search-and-can't-find-it dreams I still have at times. I am struggling to remember exactly what I experienced tonight. Though I cannot recall the details, the sense I get, the vague remembering is that I-cannot-accomplish-it-and-I-am-a-gigantic-failure. That this posturing about speaking with God and divine messages and life transformation is bullshit. I cannot do it; all of the pain I experienced on this journey of re-membering who I am, of becoming who I choose to be is in vain. It does not work, or rather I cannot work it, I am a failure at it. My life has not really changed; I am bullshitting myself. I am delusional after all. I am a failure.

I can't believe I am still experiencing this madness at this juncture in my journey. I thought I had overcome this fear, gotten past the terror of not-enoughness, of unrealized self, of failure. But here I am again. Or still.

A quote from Marianne Williamson comes to mind—"A miracle is a shift in perspective from fear to love." I think about the section in *Conversations with God* where Neale Donald Walsch talks about fear being the polar opposite of love. Explaining there are only two real states of being—fear and love. I know this. I say it often. But it occurs to me now that I really don't get it. I know it, but I don't KNOW it. It is still concept to me, not yet my experience, and I know it is when concept becomes experience that I am saved.

Help me God, I whisper. How is it that love is the opposite of fear? I know I am love. But what do I love, who do I love, how do I love to the extent that I do not experience the hell that is fear? I know not to disparage this fear, I know to embrace it for it is what is at this moment. And I know to embrace and be grateful for everything in my life at this moment, for I have drawn each thing I experience to myself and I see in each a divine opportunity to decide and demonstrate who I am, who I choose to be. I am trying not to resist it, for what I resist persists. This I know. So I embrace this nightmare of fear, I do. I have turned on the light and am fully facing it for I want it to disappear.

Help me, God. Help me re-member what I must so that I disappear this.

It is now Monday morning, 4:45 am. Tomorrow, Tuesday, is the day I have committed to my friend, and then to others to have completed this book. He has been counting down the days. Tomorrow I will not have completed the book. Tomorrow I am planning to lie to him; to tell him it is finished, that I have accomplished my goal, that I am not full of bullshit as he feared. Tomorrow it will be official. I am a failure. Again. And he will know it for sure. And he will leave me for good. And I deserve it. I had my chance and I blew it.

Okay, God. So who do I have to love to get some help around here?

Yourself.

What? I have been reciting that affirmation you gave me about the book: "I love myself enough to tell my story. Without attachment to outcome, without attachment to the past, and without even attachment to the story." I have been saying it.

Then why does it matter how long it takes?

Because I've been dicking around (sorry) with this for years. Because without a deadline it is just a pipe dream. Because I quit my job to do this and I am running out of money so I have to get this done. Because I need to prove to myself, to him, to others, that I am not just a talker. Because I have to have a way to measure my progress so I don't just diddle around. Because I don't want to be a failure.

But you feel like a failure anyway. The book will be finished when it is finished.

But you are the one who has been pushing me, imploring me to get the book done. I looked back in my journal. Over and over you tell me to write the book.

And so you are.

But you had a sense of urgency around it. And I am back on it. I am writing. I am doing it again.

So what is the problem? You are working on it. But know that you are working on it in fear, not in love. Do you see?

No I don't see. How do I write the book "in love"?

You are shifting to fear again, Susan. You have noticed it. You have spoken to yourself over the last few days about it. So many of your recent thoughts are angry thoughts, critical thoughts, judgment thoughts, failure thoughts. There is much you have picked up again. Here is the opportunity, the grand opportunity to choose again. To choose love. Writing this book is to be a journey of love, Susan. Not a painful, stressful, anxiety-ridden exercise in fear. You fear you are not capable, you fear the outcome, you fear missing the deadline, you fear inadequacy ... This is to be a love journey of a sacred soul.

Sorry, God, but this seems very sunshiny and idealistic and totally unreal. Editors give you deadlines. There are parameters, standards.

Which editor is giving you a deadline, Susan? What demands are being made of you regarding the book save those you put on yourself? You know what to do. Let go of the self-constraints. Free yourself to tell the story. You are already free to do so. Love yourself enough to enjoy this journey of love. Realign your thoughts with the Love you are. It is okay. Relax and enjoy the journey.

But I'm running out of money. How will I live? How will I eat? What if my friend leaves me for good?

Remember I told you this phase of your journey is about life source and life style? A job is not your source; you and I are your source. And if he leaves, he leaves. You know he is doing what he knows to do to help you stay on track. Your worry about this is fear. Do you choose a life style of fear? Relax. You fear because you are attached to process and you are attached to outcome. Love is not attached to process or outcome. Let go. You know who you are and you know who I am. And I tell you, you are right where you need to be in your life right at this moment.

Here's what I am coming to know: This journey is about re-membering love. Over and over again. Re-membering I am love. And demonstrating the Love I am in thought and word and deed. Again and again. And the essence of this is loving myself, which is loving God, which is loving myself, which is loving God. The core of this is knowing that God and I are one. And God and I are one with all that is. And loving God is loving myself is loving everyone because we are all one.

When I forget this I lapse into judgment and criticism and self-doubt, the hell of fear. When I re-member—

salvation, heaven, joy. I am so grateful God re-minds me I am love as often as I need re-minding. And I am so thankful that each time I forget, She gives me another opportunity to choose again, to create myself anew. So today, once again I choose love. And tomorrow? Tomorrow, even when the deadline slips, even if I skip the gym, or eat too much cake, or forget to make the phone call, tomorrow I choose love. I choose to love myself, God-in-me, this process, knowing that love casts out fear. Tomorrow I will not be afraid.

YOU KNOW, WHAT'S HIS NAME ...

The golden years have come at last
The golden years can kiss my ...
∞ Dr. Suess on Aging (Author unknown)

I am in the bookstore, hoping a change in venue will help me break through the fortress of fear I have constructed in my mind as I quickly approach my self-imposed deadline for completing the manuscript for this book. I diddle around with my laptop at a table in the store's café, searching for inspiration, for the right words, for something that will incite the flurry of thoughts flowing onto page I experience when I am in my writing zone. Nothing. A song wafts from the speakers piping music from the CD section. The voice sounds vaguely familiar, and I struggle to remember the artist I think I recognize. I can actually feel my brain searching its database for the name.

I hate that feeling. And then, yes! The name comes to me. I remember. Whew! I am not losing my mind, devolving into Alzheimer's. I abandon writing for the day, pack my laptop and head for the music section. I ask the cashier about the song's artist. It is not who I think it is, but that's okay. I peruse the CDs while listening to the beautiful voice on the speaker. A different clerk replaces the first and I approach her and tell her how much I like the music. I start to tell her the artist sounds so much like ... Damn! Just that quickly I have forgotten the singer's name again. My brain searches itself in vain but cannot retrieve it. I am frustrated; it's on the tip of my tongue. I make a quip to the clerk about old age and memory loss and move on. I wrack my brain as I leave the store and head home.

There! I remember. The name leaps into my consciousness as I pull into a parking space. Whew! I am saved again. I get out of the car and walk to my front door. I reach for the doorknob and the name. It is gone again, that quickly. Oh my God, I've lost it again—the name and my mind, I am thinking. I try to recall the name intermittently throughout the evening and into the night. I turn off my bedside lamp in the wee hours of the morning and lay my head on my waiting pillow. And there it is, the name comes to me in a flash. I immediately reach for the lamp. I pull out a Post It from my drawer and write the name on the fluorescent yellow square. Having outsmarted my flagging memory, I turn out the light again and fall peacefully asleep.

I really hate that feeling, that forgetting and trying to remember that seems to more and more frequently afflict me and those in my cohort. Our conversations are now animated by the snapping of fingers as we try to recall … something, the scrunch of foreheads in concentration, and the gentle pounding on those same foreheads as we attempt to dislodge the desired information from our stubborn brains. Every discussion is peppered with the sound bites of memory loss—"uhh, you remember; you know, what's-his-name; umm, I can't think of it right now, but it will come to me …" The brain searching, searching, reaching in vain for that speck of information, the retrieval of which assures us we are not losing our minds. I hate that feeling.

   I do not like that feeling as I travel this spiritual journey either. The reaching for something I vaguely remember, something I know is the answer. If I can just recall it, I will be saved. I had it before, I'm sure I did, because I was in peace, in joy. But I have forgotten, and have lapsed once again into fear, doubt, anxiety, dis-ease. Oh, there! I have it. Ode to Joy! I have re-membered, and I am whole again—re-membered. And then tomorrow, or the next week, or sometimes, the next hour, I forget. And the fear re-surfaces. And God has to re-mind me; either directly or through circumstances, experiences, other people. At times She reiterates what She has spoken to me/in me over and over, thousands of times. And in some instances it is a re-minding of something buried deep, deep within my psyche, something I am just coming to know. But over and over God re-minds me—who I am, who I said I choose to be. God re-minds me what really matters along the journey, how life really works, and I am saved again.

   I know on this journey, in contrast to our physical cycle, I will come to re-member more and more and forget less and less as I surrender to my oneness with God-in-me. As I allow myself to become more and more conscious of who He is and who I am. I know I will experience the peace, the love, the joy I am for longer and longer periods of time. Until I am in that perpetual consciousness of oneness with God that is love, that is home. But until then, whenever I forget and then re-member, I will turn on the light, no matter the hour and pull out my pad.

It is a day later and I have not yet forgotten that artist's name. I wrote it down. There is something about writing it down that, for me, more securely locks "knowing" into my memory, my heart. And if I do forget, I take comfort in knowing I can open the drawer and pull out that yellow Post It note and be re-minded.

I think about those dear souls who really do have dementia. I have seen news articles, heard stories of sweet senior citizens who have wandered from their houses and have forgotten the way home. Sometimes they have walked or driven for miles, for days, forgetting where home is, searching for home. And sometimes they are right in their own living rooms, but have forgotten they are home.

This is why I have begun to write my story, to scribe my journey. Until that day when I am in continual awareness of my oneness with God, not just conceptually, but experientially, I pull out my notes on the journey and God re-minds me. Each time I forget and fall into fear, God re-minds me. Until I need no more re-minding. Until I re-member with an infinite divine knowing what I always knew. Until I am where I have never really left. Until I am home.

SAVE ME

No one saves us but ourselves. No one can and no one may. We ourselves must walk the path..
∞ Buddha

I am not here to fix you or to save you, God tells me. You do not need fixing, and you save yourself.

But you are God, I reply incredulously. That's what You *do* – You save people.

Susan, you save yourself. Hear me. Each time you re-member who you are and live it, you are saved. Each time concept becomes your reality, the theoretical becomes experiential, you are saved. Each time God-in-concept, Love-in-concept becomes your own truth, you are saved. Do you see? You are saved as these abstract concepts of your highest self, your God self, become your lived experience. Thus you re-member. You begin to put the pieces of yourself together again. Though in actuality, you have never not been together, you have never been fragmented, you have never been separated from yourself, i.e. from me. This is all illusion. You are saved as you re-member you have never not been saved.

Help me understand, God.

Susan, salvation is a journey, not a destination. You don't get *there*; there is no there to get to. The journey, your journey, is about choosing and becoming, creating and living, thus re-membering. When you do this with intention, it is a sacred act, a divine undertaking. But, make no mistake about it, you do this, whether you know it or not. Whether you do so consciously or not. Whether in this phase of your journey or not.

I think about this. There was a time when I sought men I thought could "save" me.

I sat down with my former husband a few days ago. I had unfinished emotional business, and I suspect he did also, though he would never admit it. There was stuff I still could not wrap my brain around. And anyone who really knows me knows I am not satisfied with my own conjecture, guessing about what was/what is happening. I must think it through, work it through, talk it through, write it through until I have some level of comfort with the answer or the lesson or the re-membering. This is part of my pathology.

Seventeen years of relationship, I knew this man like the back of my hand. I knew his ego issues and needs, I could spot the guilty look on his face, could identify a mile away his mental maneuverings. And yet I wanted to know, needed to know on a deeper level what was really going on underneath with some of the ways he behaved, the things he did, the words he said or did not say. Who was he really, and why, honestly, did he do some of the things he did? And I wanted to understand myself in the relationship, who I was and why I behaved in the manner I did. And why I came to be the mad woman I was.

I became angry with this, my third husband, before we even stood at the altar in Las Vegas and recited our vows. He was eighteen years older than I, a charismatic man, verbose, and tended toward hyperbole, seemingly confident of his many pronouncements of "fact" about the world. This man had the answers; he knew how life worked and how to work life. And I believed him. I felt I was clueless, but I could learn from him and we could build something beautiful together.

Over time, after trying in vain to reconcile the disconnect between his words and the reality of his/our life, I began to suspect, and then knew with certainty, that he was himself struggling to make sense of the world. He knew no more than I did. He could not save me. And I became angry, seething underneath, though trying to hold it together on the surface. But, maybe I was wrong. I would go through with the marriage anyway. I was profoundly disappointed. I had been lied to, duped. I would have to save myself. Again. Or find someone else who could.

I was also disappointed with my second husband. I felt he knew more than I in the religious arena and could "save" me in that aspect of my life. The results of that belief were more disastrous than I can say. And now God tells me he himself, God, does not save me. What is it with the men in my life? Men are supposed to save you. They are supposed to be the heroes in a sister's life. My father, my husbands, my God -- why can no one save me? I'm tired of trying to save myself. I'm tired.

This is the journey, God tells me. No one saves you, but you yourself.

It has taken me over a half century to know, to remember this truth. Though it was over a year after I left the marriage, I am glad I initiated a meeting with my former husband to talk and try to wrap up unfinished emotional business. When I left the others, I moved speedily away, wanting to end connection with them immediately. This time, I knew better. This time, I was not a mad woman, and I wanted to proceed from the marriage in love and without anger. This time I wanted to understand and to forgive and be forgiven. Though there were many issues in this and my other marriages that led to their demise, this time I know I was wrong for wanting these men to do something they could not do; for wanting them to save me. So I ask the men in my life to forgive me for my madness, and I forgive them for theirs.

I could talk about some of the things my husbands did in my marriages, but their stuff is now between them and God. I leave that behind and move forward in God. I must save myself. God re-minds me that He and I are one, and we are more than equal to the task. And that salvation is a joyous journey. And that I know all I need to know at this time, and when I need to know more, He will re-mind me. And that salvation is about love—loving God, loving myself, loving all. And that this journey of love is a no-brainer. I do not have to work and toil and suffer for salvation. It is a process, a journey of supreme love. God is love and I am love. I've got this.

OTHER PEOPLE'S CHILDREN (or THE SHIT THAT WEIGHS YOU DOWN)

You wanna fly, you got to give up the shit that weighs you down.
∞ Toni Morrison, *Song of Solomon*

You know the friend you want to care for your kids if something happens to you? The one you would trust with your babies' lives? I am not that friend.

I spent time with a girlfriend's teenage daughter yesterday. What was I thinking? My friend, whom I love dearly, is in *that* phase of her life. You know, that phase where you are juggling single parenting, a high pressure job, life decisions, big purchases, handling business. I remember being there. So when my friend had taken several hours off work to handle business transactions and her daughter needed to go to a doctor's appointment the next day, I volunteered to take her.

Her daughter, at barely 18 and a senior in high school, knows everything about everything, argues about everything, and contradicts me about everything. Typically with attitude. You know, a teenager. But I had forgotten what it is like to parent a teenage girl; my only daughter is now 27, an adult out on her own.

This teenager beside me in my car is alternately an adult ("I am 18, you know"), and a child, indignantly demanding her mother buy or give her what she wants, including a car. Almost every statement she speaks to me begins with either "Yeah, but …" or "No, but …" She has "yeah butted" me through breakfast at Denny's, her doctor's appointment, and our trip to the pharmacy to pick up her prescription, "no, butted" me through my runs to the gas station, and through the car wash. By early afternoon, I want to cry. Or to commit murder, or suicide. Or better yet a murder/suicide.

She "word for words" me on every topic. And she will not stop. After she endlessly argues with me about love relationships (not that she's even been on a date), I order, "Stop talking. Just stop talking!" "Yeah, but …" she keeps going. "Close your mouth," I all but shout. "No, but …" I stop the car at a red light. I want to kick open the passenger side door from the inside and shove the teenager beside me out into the busy street. "If you don't stop arguing with me I will stop this car and put you out like I have done with my own daughter!" I finally command, because I am the mature one. "Yeah, but you can't do that to other people's children," she retorts smugly. "I would have to call the police."

She does not know me. She does not know that the mad woman I used to be is lurking dangerously close to the surface of my "cool Aunty" persona. She does not know I have stopped the car on several occasions and put my own mouthy teenage daughter out so that I would not murder her within the confines of my BMW or Audi. Blood stains, you know. She does not know I am dangerously close to doing so with her.

"What are you going to tell the police?" I demand. "You are 18 years old now, remember? Technically an adult. They would laugh at you," I say, because I am the mature one. I feel the blood pumping in my temples, the signs of an impending headache, and swing the car into a Wendy's parking lot. Her mouth is closed for once, pondering this information, her inability to charge me (or her mother, I suspect) with child abuse or neglect, because she is technically no longer a child. "I am going into this Wendy's to get a drink so I can take some medicine for the headache I've gotten fooling around with you all day" I tell the woman-child beside me, because I am the mature one. "Would you like a Frosty?" Of course she would.

I return to the car and take the three Ibuprofen remaining in the bottle in my purse. The teenager beside me is now remorseful for having caused me pain. "Ms. Susan, I'm sorry for arguing with you all day. Can I hang out with you the rest of the day? I don't want to be home *all alone.*" (Cue the violins.) Yeah, right. Her behind is going home. "Your behind is going home," I tell her because I am the mature one. She sighs. "Well, okay, but after you get over your headache, maybe next week, can I come over to your house and we can cook together?" "Of course you can,

Sweetie," I tell her. I am lying. She cannot come to my house and cook with me. Ever. Well, not until the terms "yeah, but …" and "no, but …" have been removed from her vocabulary. Not until she comes to know that she knows almost nothing. Not until she has enough self-discipline or common sense to shut her mouth when she sees I am a woman on the edge. Not until she is 35.

I drop her at her house at 2:45 pm and smile and wave, smile and wave until she closes the door safely behind her. Then I drive like a bat out of hell to my own house. I do not stop at the mailbox to retrieve my mail, I do not hang up my jacket in the hall closet, I do not even stack my decorative pillows neatly on the floor as I usually do. I shove the pillows to the other side of the bed, kick off my shoes, and climb in fully clothed. It is 3:00 in the afternoon and I am going to bed, exhausted and undone by a teenage girl who was acting like, well, a teenage girl. I do not care that this is ridiculous, I pull the covers over my head and go to sleep.

I awaken two hours later feeling refreshed. And grateful. I have not shoved someone else's child into traffic, the headache did not take hold, and I am happy I am not my friend, the mother of two teenagers. I feel strangely … free!

And with that word, free, I know there is a spiritual message in this situation. God has been speaking to me lately about freedom, though until this moment my own freedom felt more conceptual than experiential. That in itself is a bit odd since people see me as the epitome of freedom. In the recent past I have walked away from a marriage that no longer worked for me (the third one I have left), quit a job that no longer fulfilled me, and am completing this book.

Yet I did not feel free. And God, a few months ago, began to speak to me/within me about the agenda of my soul as I considered leaving my job. The agenda of your soul, God told me, is to be free—free to love, free to touch the lives of others, free to write, free to read. "What do you mean, free?" I asked, thinking of my potential lost income. "How will I live? How will I eat? How will I be in the relationships I choose?" If you are not free you cannot do any of these things, God answered me. If your mind is constrained and your heart is limited and holding. It is only in being free that the things you seek will come to you. This is my way. In this way, in my way, your financial needs will be met, you will pay off your debt as you desire, you will be financially free. Do you not know who I am? Do you not know who you are?

"Well, yes, but how will this work? I don't understand. Is this you, God, or is it my imagination? Am I just trying to justify a hasty decision to leave my job?"

Be still, God tells me. Relax. Your glory, your joy is fulfilled in me; not in working a job, not in being in a relationship. Though you can choose these things if you wish. Step out in faith and be, do, and have that which your soul desires, longs for. Your soul desires to fully express itself as your highest conception of yourself, your life. And it must be free to do so. Set yourself free from the relationship, from the job and you will freely receive/experience that which you choose to experience. If you are bound to them, you will never freely experience them. You will always be worrying about how to keep them, whether you will lose them. Do you see?

"No, I am not sure I do?"

The job is not your livelihood; it is not your source. The relationship is not your salvation. Set your soul free to live and to love. True freedom is an act of radical surrender, as is love.

"What does that mean?"

To experience freedom you must let go of that which keeps you bound. You are already free. But you do not experience your freedom because you have created attachments. Attachments to people, places, things, outcomes, processes. Expectations. So you do not feel free.

But how does this work? We, I, have responsibilities. And yes, attachments. Like relationships, like jobs, like financial obligations.

And you live them all in fear. You do not trust that I've got your back. That my love holds you, keeps you. You are afraid you will lose what you have, or that you will not get what you choose, or that what you have will change into a form you do not desire. You are afraid what this loss means about you. You are ultimately afraid you will be alone and unloved and unsustained.

"Well, yes."

You cannot experience freedom in fear. Freedom can only be felt in love. And I do not mean in an intimate love relationship with another as you define it. I mean divine love, the love that is oneness with me. This love cannot be found with a man, Susan, or with a job, or with an amount of money, or even in writing a book. You can have these things if you choose, but to be free while having them—

that is the journey. You will not experience real peace, lasting peace, if you are not free. And you cannot experience real freedom if you are not love.

"So that's why I, sooner or later, feel inner turmoil again, unsatisfied, restless, even when I have what I want?"

Yes. The peace is not in having the thing or the person. The peace is in having it in freedom, ultimately, in love.

"So, what do I have to do to experience ongoing peace, love, freedom?"

Re-member who you are. And let go. They go hand in hand. You cannot know who you really are, and consistently live it in peace, if you are attached to/seek fulfillment from the situation or the person.

"But how? How do I let go?"

You know the answer to this, Susan. One thought at a time, one decision at a time, one breath at a time.

"Yes. Thank you God."

I don't know how I would do this, this letting go, if I had dependent children, teenagers. I can't even imagine how that would look. But thankfully, I am free of teenagers. And God tells me I am free to live the life I choose. I just have release the things that block my full experience of my freedom. I have to let go. This I know. I have even written about letting go. But I am still working on this, and I am determined to experience the continual peace that this freedom affords. "Know you are already free," God tells me. This is the journey. Wow! What could I accomplish, what could I be, if surrender to this truth and know, really know, that I am free?

QUEEN OF HEARTS

Tell your heart that the fear of suffering is worse than the suffering itself. And that no heart has ever suffered when it goes in search of its dreams, because every second of the search is a second's encounter with God and with eternity.
∞ Paulo Coelho, *The Alchemist*

Today I am in joy. This is unusual for me. Not so much the joy part; as I progress on this journey, more and more often I consciously choose to live in joy, to be joy. I mean, the writing about it part. I usually write when I am in pain, fear, dis-ease. It is in these unhappy states I have most opened myself to God's love, to God re-minding me who I am, who I said I choose to be. But I am changing. I am slowly coming to live and learn in joy and peace and love. These have become my truths, so today I am in joy.

Today, in response to some unknown prompting, I feel for my heart, patting my chest with my right hand, grade school style. I feel something unusual. I feel ... a steady beat, good, strong like everything is okay. Like the pain I've felt there so often is missing. Like I am day-by-day letting go of fear and surrendering to love and trust and peace. This feels good. Today I say from experience, not just hope, "my heart is sound."

Your heart is sound, Susan. God has spoken this to me, over and over, when I have cried out that my heart is breaking and that I am in indescribable pain. Today I feel for my heart and the jagged broken edges are not there. Even though everything did not go as planned in my life today. Even though something I wanted to happen today did not manifest, my heart is sound. I am amazed at this and I realize something has shifted in me. It has begun to work. I have been practicing letting go of attachment to outcome, of attachment to how I think the process should work. And today, though my day did not go as I wished, I am not broken by disappointment. I am astonished by this, then doubtful.

I pat my chest once more, just to be sure, searching in vain for the pain, for the hollow feeling of fear I am so used to. For the familiar halting stutter, the sharp ragged edges— a testimony to my brokenness. Instead I feel the harmony, the rhythm of love, of oneness. This is foreign to me, this soundness of heart, and I am filled with wonder.

Your heart is sound, God has assured me again and again. A statement of fact to Him, but to me, a promise I could not even begin to fathom. How would that feel—a sound heart? And now, today, I reached for my heart, and for the first time in a long time, I recognize a perfect, strong rhythm. It feels like blessed assurance that God's promises are true, unfailing. It feels like the triumph of love over fear. Like freedom. Like joy. Like salvation.

IT'S NOT ABOUT THE MAN

For you see, in the end, it is between you and God. It was never between you and them anyway.
∞ Mother Teresa

*I*t's not about the man, Susan, God tells me over and over again. If you make it about a man you will surely feel as if you lose your mind.

This as I am writhing in pain, desperate and alone. Again. This as my heart aches, as not-enoughness grips and wrings and tears at it until I am in a ball on my sofa, then on the floor, sobbing, sobbing.

The man, the relationship, God tells me calmly, gently, is just context for your journey. This is not about a man; this is about you.

On some level I know this, of course. I know this angst I am experiencing is not really or just about the painful ending (sort of) of a dysfunctional relationship I was desperate to hold onto. Something deeper is happening here. But I am not yet tuned in enough to my spiritual knowing about the relationship to really get it at this point, though I am struggling to do so. To see it as the on-again, off-again, on-again (sort of), struggle of two hurting individuals desperately seeking to be enough for each other, for themselves, for the task of relating to another on an authentic level, a fulfilling level. In a way that doesn't scare them to death for fear of not being enough. For fear of being abandoned in a lonely meaningless world.

I am beginning to sense, just at the periphery of my awareness, that this is about the individual journeys of two sacred souls searching for meaning on their own, seeking oneness with themselves, with the world, with God. Trying to get home. The man (at least from my standpoint) is not really the issue. The relationship is context. This is about the journey; my journey.

But at this point, I am just barely, fleetingly, becoming conscious of this. I am struggling to re-member. All I really know at this point is I am alone in pain. And that the black hole of emptiness within me threatens to expand outward until it consumes me and returns me to days when thin brown children dance on the rim of reality. All I really know is I am losing my mind. And God, being God, being Love, re-minds me dozens, hundreds, thousands of times – it is not about the man. It is about me; my journey of becoming, of expressing, who I am, who I choose to be. It is not about the man. Until this knowing begins to take root in me.

When I was a mad woman I thought it was about him—the way we he treated me, the way he spoke to me. The way I fought back. The way I felt when I was with him.

The way I wanted him, wanted this so badly. Wanted this oneness, this validation, this salvation. The way I felt when he chose me, or did not choose me. The way I walked away or not. The way I hated myself because I was not good enough. I thought it was about him. I thought it was about them all—the husbands, the other relationships with the men in my life. I thought it was about them.

Every relationship I have had has been based on fear. Especially my relationship with God. God never gives me what I desire, I have feared. I am not worthy, not good enough. And my relationship with myself is a mirror of my relationship with God. Fear; self-loathing; punitive; undeserving of real joy, real fulfillment, real peace. And of course, this fear is reflected in my relationships with others —friends, lovers, colleagues. FEAR.

I raised my children in utter fear, and related to them in that manner. I was afraid I could not succeed at this very adult task—I would screw up these wonderful little people given into my care, I would make wrong decisions in our lives, I would mess up and ruin them. I went into relationships with men in fear. Was I good enough to keep them, could they/would they save me? I just knew I needed to be saved. Fear undergirded every relationship because I felt I was not enough. And I looked for them—the men, the colleagues, even the children – to validate my worth. I thought it was about me and them.

But God finally, finally got through to me when, after years— decades—of madness, anger, terror threatened to drown the life out of me, I surrendered to the re-membering. Like I had been holding myself under water, and just as I give in to the certainty of death, I re-member and lift my head. God re-minds me, had been re-minding me, and I finally give in to the knowing, and I am saved. It is not about the man, the men. Any of them. It was never between me and them. It is about my journey. It is between me and God.

Here is what I am coming to know: The relationship with the man is a reflection of my relationship, my oneness with God, with myself. And as I re-member this incredible divine love that God is, I love myself with blessed assurance that this love never fails. I am love because God is love and because God and I are one. I am not fear, the basis of my madness. So whatever form the relationship with the man takes, however it proceeds, it is not a failure, and I am not a failure. With this divine love, I trust God-in-me, I trust myself, and I trust the process of life She has set in motion. I know with divine knowing I will be okay.

The man, the relationship is context. The journey is about re-membering who I am. And who I am is One Divine Love. It is about the triumph of love. The divine love relationship with God, with myself and with all of life. One Divine love, the opposite of the fear-filled relationships I have always created and experienced. This is what my soul desires—this is the journey. The journey of re-membering the Love I am. This is what my soul seeks, and what I am creating. My very first self/God/man relationship without fear.

The man, the relationship with the man, is context for my journey of re-membering and living my truth. They present opportunities for me to decide, declare, and demonstrate who I am, who I choose to be. I re-member my oneness with God and all of life, and I choose to live the Love I am. And that love includes loving myself because I now know my worth. And loving the man because I re-member his. And knowing we and God are one, I love the man as I love myself as I love God. Without fear or anger.

I am no longer a mad woman. I am love, I am a lover. And I now know this has little to do with the man or the situation at hand. The man may change, the situation almost certainly will. It is not that the man does not matter. He is a sacred soul in his own right, and a divine partner for some portion of my life journey. But my journey is not primarily about those who are divinely drawn to me (or I to them) along the way. It is not about the man or the colleagues, or even the children. It is about me and God. And re-membering/knowing who I am, and becoming who I choose to be. This is the journey.

GOING HOME

The soul doesn't evolve or grow, it cycles and twists, repeats and reprises, echoing ancient themes common to all human beings. It is always circling home ... Its odyssey is a drifting at sea, a floating toward home, not an evolution toward perfection
∞ Thomas Moore, Original Self

What is it? I am asking God. What is the knowing or the re-membering or the attitude, or the reality that, once I attain it, will get me there and keep me there? Is it salvation, enlightenment, nirvana I seek? Is that the state of experiencing perpetual oneness with God, a continuous state of joy and satisfaction and well-being? Is that home?

...

He said she slept over last night, but they did not have sex. He said he told her he was tired, told her he did not feel like it. Then he told her this morning that he could not sleep well with her in the bed; it wasn't comfortable. He laughed and told me he really slept like a rock. We made love. I could not really relax into it. I was tense. I remember when he began giving me those excuses. He said he is slowly pulling away from her, doesn't take her places like he did in the beginning. Said she will begin to get the message. Said this is better than just cutting the relationship off at once. He said as she gets the message, he will then tell her it is not working out. I remember when he "handled" me this way, after a few months into our relationship. I feel for her. I feel for myself. Not exactly sorry for her or myself; she knows he is pulling away, as I knew. She is not a victim and neither was I.

...

Men talk too much. Maybe women do also. Perhaps we should all just shut up. Maybe then we could better maintain the illusion that we are not who we really are. Not reveal our real selves because our real selves are profoundly lacking, and self-serving, and scary and not enough. Not ever enough. Not reveal that we are bad underneath. Is he bad underneath? I know he feels he is. He has told me this on more than one occasion, though not recently. "I am a bad person," he has confessed. "I am evil."

And me, I am figuring out how not to talk so much, how to try harder to hide my "real self"—my insecurities, my fears, my own manipulative tendencies, my own not enoughness, so I can have the relationships I want, the things I want. Perhaps we are all trying to get the best deal for ourselves before we check out of here. To get what we feel will make us happy. We are all using each other, I think, to get to happy.

You see, I am trying to "manipulate" him to choose me, because I think having him will make me "happy". That, for me, is getting the best deal for myself. This I feel will make me happy. So I cook for him, seek his sage advice on everything. Try to make him happy. All to "get him" because this will make me happy. Then I will work hard to try to keep him so I can continue to be happy. Then I will realize I am not happy. Then I will leave him. And I will start all over again with the next person or thing I think will make me happy. Or I build the house I really want, and buy the BMW, but sooner or later I realize I am not happy. So I sabotage those situations, "leaving them." And I look for "happiness" in the next experience or relationship or job, or the book, or whatever is next. I spend my whole life chasing "happy," the best deal for myself. And I am always disappointed. What am I doing? What are we all doing? God, what the hell?

Today I recognize the malaise. Again. I am not really happy. And I have done the things I thought would make me happy: I left the husband, quit the job, am working on the book, the relationship is on the way. But there is that malaise. Again. Or still, always just under the surface. The point is none of this, the things I wanted or wanted to do, have ever really eradicated this malaise, this un-ease, this sense of, not sadness exactly, but un-happiness. Am I just never satisfied? Am I clinically depressed? Am I always hunting for the next person or thing, the next high? Why am I never happy for long? Why can't I just relax into wherever I am, whatever I am doing at the time, into the relationship as it is? i.e. why cannot I maintain happy? I can certainly understand why people self-medicate, drink, or drug. If there were a pill for this, I would take it.

Is it as the Bible seems to teach us that the flesh wants "happy," but the soul, the spirit wants "home"? So we should subdue the flesh, destroying its desires so we can get "home"? At one point in my life I bought into this. Then, no, this is bullshit. Now, I am not sure what the answer is. Does it have to be either/or? Either happy *or* home? I don't think so, but, what do I know?

This I do know. God has been speaking to me over the last year or so, telling me—re-minding me—of that which, on some level I already know. Re-minding me that it is not about the man, not about the job, or the money, or the house, or even really the book. I can have those things if I choose, She tells me, and that's fine, but they are not the point of this adventure, this odyssey called my life. They are just context for this phase of the journey of my soul. And the journey of my soul is about home—re-minding me, awakening me to home. Not home as in a destination, a place to get to, but the journey itself is homecoming. The process is homecoming. Coming home to a place we have never actually left.

But we have forgotten this. It is like the Tao of the Wizard of Oz. Dorothy, after all, never left home. Her journey was all a dream from which she awakened, finding herself still at home. We, like Dorothy, have never really left home, have never left God, for we are infinitely and only One with Him. But we have forgotten this, since the dream of our lives seems so real. And on a deep, deep level, we, like Dorothy, like Shirley Temple in the old movie *The Bluebird of Happiness*," like Homer in *The Odyssey*, like the

Prodigal Son of the Bible, just want to go home. But in our illusion of disconnectedness, separation, fragmentation within this dream we are dreaming, we confuse happiness with home. We struggle to find happy, because we have come to believe that that is what satisfies. But we also know, we really do, that happy is temporal, and that underneath we are seeking something else, some other state.

In his beautiful book, *In Search of Stones*, noted psychotherapist and philosopher M. Scott Peck (author of *The Road Less Traveled*), speaks of his many marital infidelities. He muses that in some way, the seeking out of these illicit liaisons, the act of consummation with one after another, was his desperate seeking for oneness with God, a burning quest for home. Bullshit, I thought when I first read this. This is just another man (as in male) using God, religion, spirituality to justify screwing around. In my second marriage, the one to the Baptist minister, I had been privy to several of these self-serving bootleg rationalizations from him, church leaders and other "religious" folk. "See, God told me …" Bullshit.

But maybe, in some sick and sad way, they, like the rest of us, are really seeking home.

Here is what I am coming to know: We cannot screw our way or buy our way, or even "love" our way home. We can never be perfect enough, ok enough, or ever "enough" for home. We just need to re-member that we are already there. This is the faith, not works, the Bible speaks of. This knowing, this divine knowing, that we have never left God and have never, ever been left by Him. This almost unbelievable assurance that God is not mad with us, is not perpetually poised to reach over the divide that separates our lowliness from His awesomeness and whack us with that rod of correction we learned about in Sunday School. This knowing that nothing, nothing can separate us from Her. Ever.

There is no me without God. And incredibly, amazingly, thankfully, there is no God without me. We are One.

The journey that is our lives is this re-membering, this consciousness, this awakening from the dream of separation. This knowing, not conceptually, not theoretically, but in "reality" that we are already home. That we have always been and will always be. Nothing, nothing separates us from the love of God. Our only "sin" is in not re-membering this. And as we re-member, as concept becomes experience, as theory becomes knowing, we are "saved," not once, but over and over and over again. And everything changes. And we begin slowly, slowly perhaps, to let go of the hunt for happiness, and to relax, be at peace, at home.

AFTERWORD

A WORD FROM OUR SPONSOR

I want to see how Love will triumph.
∞ Susan Harvey

*L*astly, God spoke with to me in a love letter. And I know in my spirit, He speaks this to you, to all of you.

My Love,

It is not about the man, or the lack thereof. It is not about the job or the kids or grandkids. It is not about the bills or the condition of the house, or your weight or wrinkles or gray hair. It is not about your education or girlfriends or salary.

It is about letting go of, surrendering, everything—every thing, every thought, every attitude, every belief—that stands between you and your experience of who you are, who you choose to be, the life you choose, the one meant for you. You will be, do, and have what you choose when you are willing to lose; not when you gain. Not when you *do* the right next thing. Do you see? When you risk losing it all. When you love and trust to the extent that you let go of that thing that you are most afraid of losing, of those things that you are most desperate to hang on to.

Let go of resistance and allow life, the process, to flow. You are at that place now. At the place of your breakthrough. If you will let go. It is okay if you do not; I will always love you. But I tell you here is the place of your breakthrough. The way is surrender. You are at the door now. The door is surrender. It is okay; I am with you. You know how much I love you. You know me, you know yourself—who I am, who you are. You know the way. Now you are ready to hear, to understand. All situations, all your life, have led you to this point—the point of now. Do you see? This is your breakthrough.

It is not about me, or the universe, denying you, withholding from you that which you choose for your life. It is about showing you the way to that which you choose. And the way is not *doing*. The way is surrender, the way is letting go. "Stripping away" is a much too action-oriented term; it connotes work. This process is more un-work, un-doing. You have always worked at things, fought, struggled. I understand you thought this was the way. It is the only way you know. And you suffered—dis-ease, fear, pain. For you never felt you could work hard enough to get what you choose, or consistently enough to keep it. And you were right. It is not about working hard or struggling, it is not about *doing*.

You will *do*, but this will be inspired doing, flowing from your being. Being-ness as you stop struggling, stop resisting, stop doing for a moment. Just be. This is the way of peace you seek. This is the way home.

As you stop resisting, stop struggling, all falls away. As you stop fighting what is, and flow with it, all rightly aligns. As you let go and learn to "lightly hold" all things in your hand, you will experience the freedom, the peace, the love you are. This is the essence of detachment. It is not about holding on for dear life; it is about letting go and allowing it to come to you, and holding it lightly.

You are full of fear. You are so afraid you will not have that which you choose, the life you choose, the way you choose – in love and peace and blessed assurance. In your way—holding tightly, desperately—you may get it, but in fear, sporadically, anxiously, stressfully, painfully. Always being afraid of losing it, always feeling unworthy of it, always on edge. And losing it again, and again. And you can continue to do this if you choose. I am with you in it all. I love you and I will never leave you. I can never leave you, for you and I are one. And I do not judge your choice. I do not judge you. I am here to re-mind you who you are and of what you are capable. You choose.

My way, you can have that which you choose—the man, the job, the family life, the abundance, the stuff of life. I am not against these things. But you will not have them in peace and joy and love until you are willing to let go, to surrender your fearful clutch on them, *until you are willing to risk all, trusting me, God-in-you; trusting yourself; and trusting the process of life.* I know this may sound counterintuitive to you. You are not used to trusting anything but yourself and your hard work, for "life" has taught you this. But trust me. I know you know this. You know this deep in your spirit, but you are afraid and so you have forgotten. Trust your deep knowing. Trust me. I am with you, you and I are one. I am Love so you are Love. You will see how love triumphs.

Eternal Love,

God

ACKNOWLEDGMENTS

I would like to acknowledge my parents, the late John and Annie McFadden, who did their best to love and protect me. And my beautiful Auntie, Daisy Granger, sojourning on this earth for almost a century. She taught me to be a lady.

I also acknowledge my sister-friends: My BFF Valerie Jackson – we struggled together and supported each other as we single-parented our babies and tried to figure out life. We shared adventures, tears, laughter, loss, and love.

And my girlfriends in Colorado Springs and around the world. Your support has been invaluable.

I love you all madly.

ABOUT THE AUTHOR

Susan Harvey has always been a seeker. She has an undergraduate degree in Philosophy and a Masters degree in Teaching and Learning. She has had careers in human resources and higher education, worked with student groups, run a woman's organization, and is a sought after speaker. She conducts workshops and training sessions on many topics, including personal mission, the spiritual journey, and transformative learning. Harvey continues her journey, blogs, coaches, trains, and writes from Colorado Springs, CO.

www.ingramcontent.com/pod-product-compliance
Lightning Source LLC
Chambersburg PA
CBHW070152100426
42743CB00013B/2884

9780692234556